Images of Sarsfield Barracks

Images of Sarsfield Barracks

Denis Carroll, Michael Deegan, Stephen Kelly & William Sheehan

Nonsuch

First published 2008

Nonsuch Publishing
73 Lower Leeson St, Dublin 2, Ireland
www.nonsuchireland.com

British Library Cataloguing in Publication Data.
A catalogue record for this book is available from the British Library.

ISBN 978 1 84588 939 5

Printed in Ireland

CONTENTS

The Memory of the Dead

Then here's their memory – may it be
For us a guiding light,
To cheer our strife for liberty,
And teach us to unite –
Through good and ill, be Ireland's still,
Though sad as theirs your fate,
And true men be you, men,
Like those of Ninety-Eight.

John Kells Ingram,
March 1843

FOREWORD

Sarsfield Barracks has always had a prominent position in the history of the city of Limerick. From construction of the barracks in 1798 to the present day, it has provided a home for many units, from the Manchester Regiment in the late 1800s to the 12th Infantry Battalion of today. This pictorial overview provides a visual history of the barracks, the units and the individuals who inhabited its parade ground and barrack rooms over many years. These images are now hopefully captured for posterity in this excellent compilation. Great credit is due to the authors of this book, whose initiative and tireless research has resulted in the production of this informative work.

Liam O'Carroll,
Lieutenant-Colonel,
Officer Commanding
12th Infantry Battalion & Sarsfield Barracks

Acknowledgements

This book would not have been possible without the contributions and efforts of the following individuals and institutions.

Firstly, we would like to take this opportunity to thank Lt-Col. Liam O'Carroll, who has supported this project since his appointment as Officer Commanding 12th Infantry Battalion, and his predecessor, Lt-Col. Matthew Murray, who gave initial permission to begin this project.

We would also like to thank the servicemen and women of the 12th Infantry Battalion and all other units serving in Sarsfield Barracks, who have helped to make this book a reality, namely: Battalion Sergeant-Major Gerry Dineen; Battalion Quartermaster Sergeant William MacNamara; Signalman Tony Deloughrey, and the Barracks Chaplain Seamus Madigan. We would also like to thank Company Quartermaster Sergeant Fr Eamonn O'Riordan for the use of his office during the period of the project.

Many individuals contributed pictures to this book, both Regulars and Reservists, and are too numerous to mention on an individual basis, nevertheless we are eternally grateful to all of them for their assistance. One individual, however, must be acknowledged for his enthusiasm, expertise, and passion for recording the photographic history of the modern barracks, and that is Company Quartermaster Sergeant Gerry Cosgrove, without whose assistance this book would not have been possible.

We would also like to thank all the ex-servicemen who helped with this book, in the selfless provision of pictures and their time in identifying units, personnel, and locations in various pictures. We would like to thank Michael O'Dwyer for his logistical support, through his company, Plant 4 Hire, and the following people and institutions, for giving assistance and in some cases permission to use their images: Gerry O'Doherty of the *The Irish Times*; the *Limerick Leader*; the *Star*; Brian Hodgkinson of the Jim Kemmy Municipal Museum (Limerick); Egleston Brothers Photography; the Mary Immaculate College Library; Michael Maguire and Mairead Downes of the Limerick City Library; the National Library of Ireland; the Military Archives of Ireland, Noreen Ellerker – St Mary's Church of Ireland Archives and the Royal Munster Fusiliers Association; the Welcome Library (London); the National Archives of the United Kingdom, and the Manchester Regimental Archives.

Finally, we would to thank all our families and friends for their support over the past year, while we worked on this book.

Denis Carroll
Michael Deegan
Stephen Kelly
William Sheehan

Introduction

We hope that this publication will make a contribution to the military history of Ireland and to the lives of all those that have served, past and present, in Sarsfield Barracks throughout the many years since it was built. It is important that the pictorial history of the Barracks is remembered and recorded not just for posterity but because it also charts Ireland's past. Many soldiers have passed through the main gates of Sarsfield Barracks to start an adventure of a lifetime, no matter what the reasons may have been initially, and have given not just honourable service to their country but also a personal commitment to themselves, their families and the wider world. We also hope that this pictorial history of Sarsfield Barracks will give everybody an understanding and an illuminating insight into what it was and is like to serve in the military, and the sense of pride, achievement and personal fulfilment that soldiers receive when reaching goals that are set to them in preparation, training, careers, duties and overseas service. The soldiers of Sarsfield Barracks have throughout the years attained the highest standards in soldiering both at home and abroad and we hope that we have brought just some of those achievements to the fore in this book. This book is not and was never intended be a definitive history of Sarsfield Barracks, as it would be impossible to record every event in this short space, but we hope that you will enjoy some of the memories that are recorded here.

We, the authors, would also like to say that our proceeds, if any, will be donated equally to the charitable organisation ONET and the Military Museum in Sarsfield Barracks. Both these causes are, in our opinion, worthy of support. Again, we would like to express our gratitude to everyone that made this possible.

The Napoleonic Wars led to a concerted effort to build many barracks and fortifications throughout the south of Ireland. Fear of a seaborne French invasion meant the port towns of Waterford, Cork and Limerick saw increases in the number of soldiers being garrisoned there. By 1807 there was a total of three barracks in Limerick City and between them they were able to accommodate nearly 3,000 troops and 216 horses.

Construction of the New Barracks (Sarsfield Barracks) may have begun in September 1795, as this was when the original lease started. The site for the New Barracks was chosen in the parish of St Michael's in Prospect Row and was leased rather than purchased. It was eleven acres one rood and thirty-six perches in size and was leased originally from J.T. Monsell. The contractor for building the barracks was John Gibson and the architect was Graham Myers Esq. On 25 February 1797, the revised cost of the New Barracks in Limerick was around £13,500 and according to the contractor John Gibson, it would double accommodation numbers for officers, privates and stabling for horses. The figure of £13,500 equates to €1.2 million, quite a substantial sum of money in 1797. The barracks was built inside a perimeter curtain wall which was built to keep soldiers in and from deserting, as well as to keep any local inquisitors out. Up until this juncture, barracks had been built mainly behind town walls, such as the those in King John's Castle, and the New Barracks represented a policy shift to concentrate the state of the military force in large numbers.

The main buildings of the New Barracks formed a square shape that centred on the parade ground, which was used for the marching and drilling of soldiers and that taught the soldiers both discipline and arms drill. The main accommodation buildings were built with limestone blocks three stories high (the stone may have been obtained from several quarries which were located nearby). In subsequent years, more buildings were added on as needs changed; a district military prison was built *c.*1845, which had fifty-nine cells. In 1865 it contained eighty-seven prisoners and a staff of a chief warden and seven wardens and servants. Cookhouses, a hospital and recreation hall were built in the 1840s, a washing house in 1852, married quarters *c.*1878 and a skittle alley and a fives court in the 1890s.

Conditions in the barracks meant having to use urinals that were located outside the sleeping quarters. There were no inside lavatories and open wooden tubs were used at night-time which were located in the corner of the room. Sewers were not yet in place because it was not until the 1860s that the implementation of sanitary conditions was addressed by the authorities. All other domestic activities were also carried out in these rooms, such as cooking, eating, sleeping, washing and the cleaning of uniforms, weapons and boots. The cooking was done in the fireplaces in the room and four-gallon iron pots, flesh forks, buckets, grates, fire shovels and tongs were the basic cooking utensils issued to a room by the ordnance department.

The New Barracks could accommodate over 500 troops, and in the event of a contingency they would double this to 1,000 soldiers, which led to crowded conditions that were ripe for any contagious diseases to spread like wildfire. Diseases such the flu, common cold, tuberculosis and measles were common. In wet weather clothes would have been hung near the fireplace to dry along clothes lines, and by 1847, a British Parliamentary report showed that nearly 87 per cent of barracks in Ireland had no washhouse for clothes and 90 per cent had no ablution house. There was little or no privacy to speak of; the rooms had high ceilings and one fireplace, which offered little or no heat for those that were not directly near it.

Over the years, many of the regiments of the British Army served at one time or another in the New Barracks, recruiting locally and providing revenue for the local economy. These British units left the Barracks to serve overseas on many occasions, in wars from Crimea to the First World War.

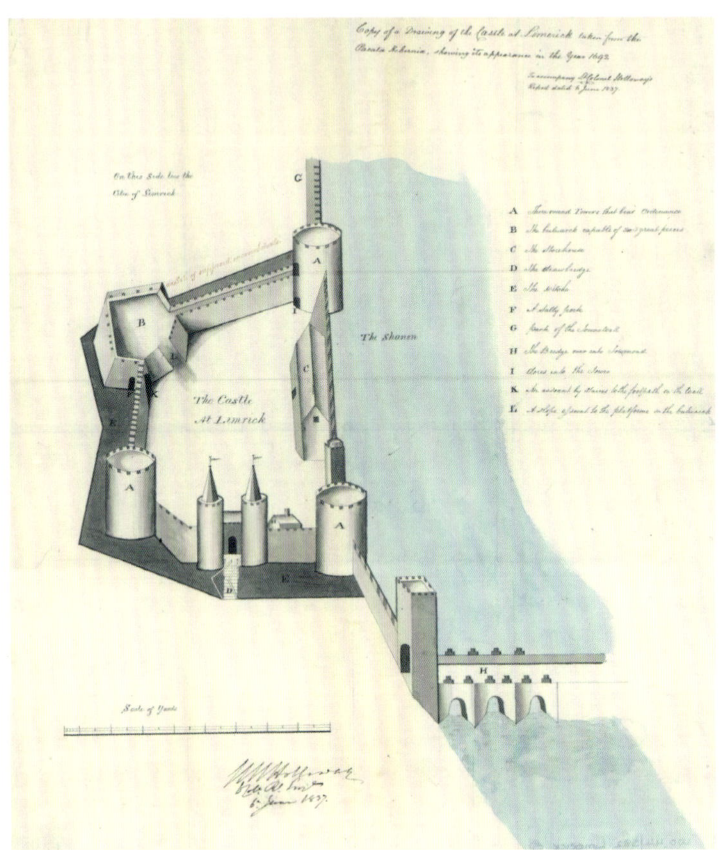

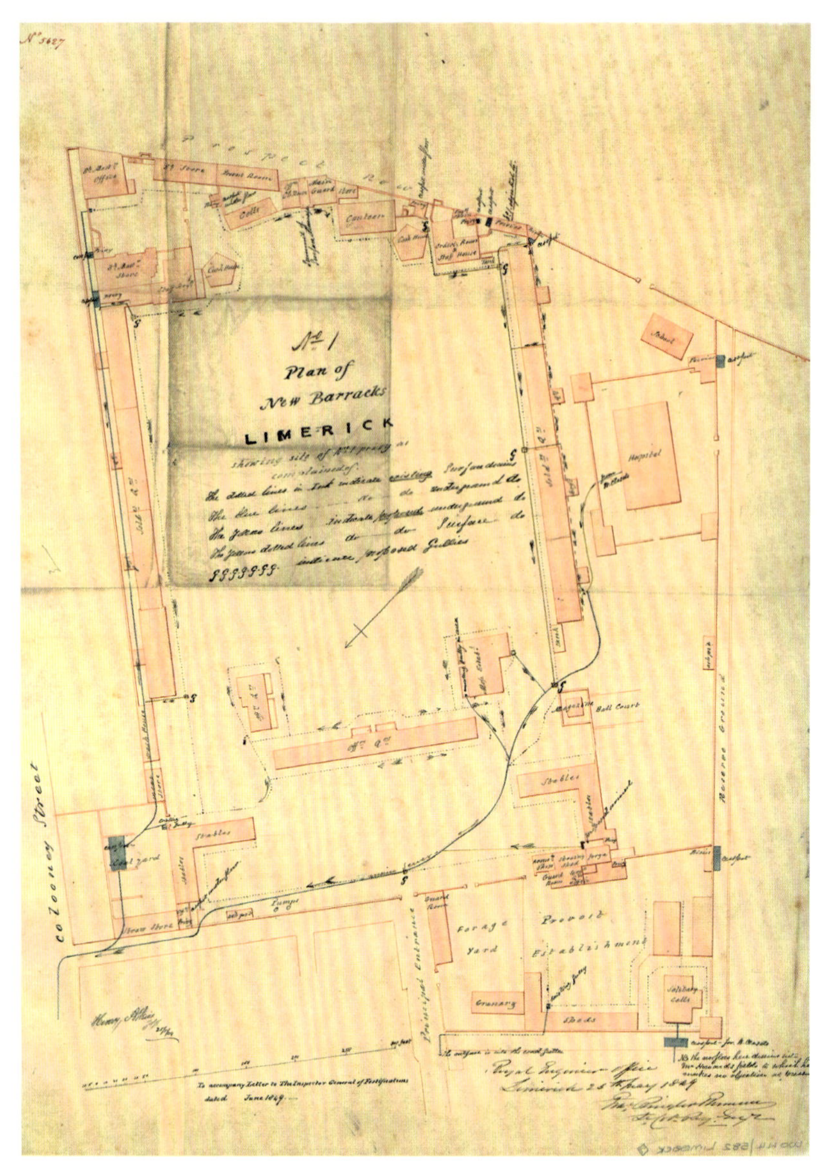

Above: Map of the Castle Barracks, produced 1837, showing the layout of the Barracks in 1692. (Courtesy of the National Archives of the United Kingdom.)

Right: Map of New Barracks, 1847. (Courtesy of the National Archives of the United Kingdom.)

Above left: The Royal Irish Fusiliers on the Square, 1880.

Above right: A drawing of the gym, New Barracks, 1884. (Courtesy of Limerick City Museum.)

Right: A plan of the gym, New Barracks, 1894. (Courtesy of the National Archives of the United Kingdom.)

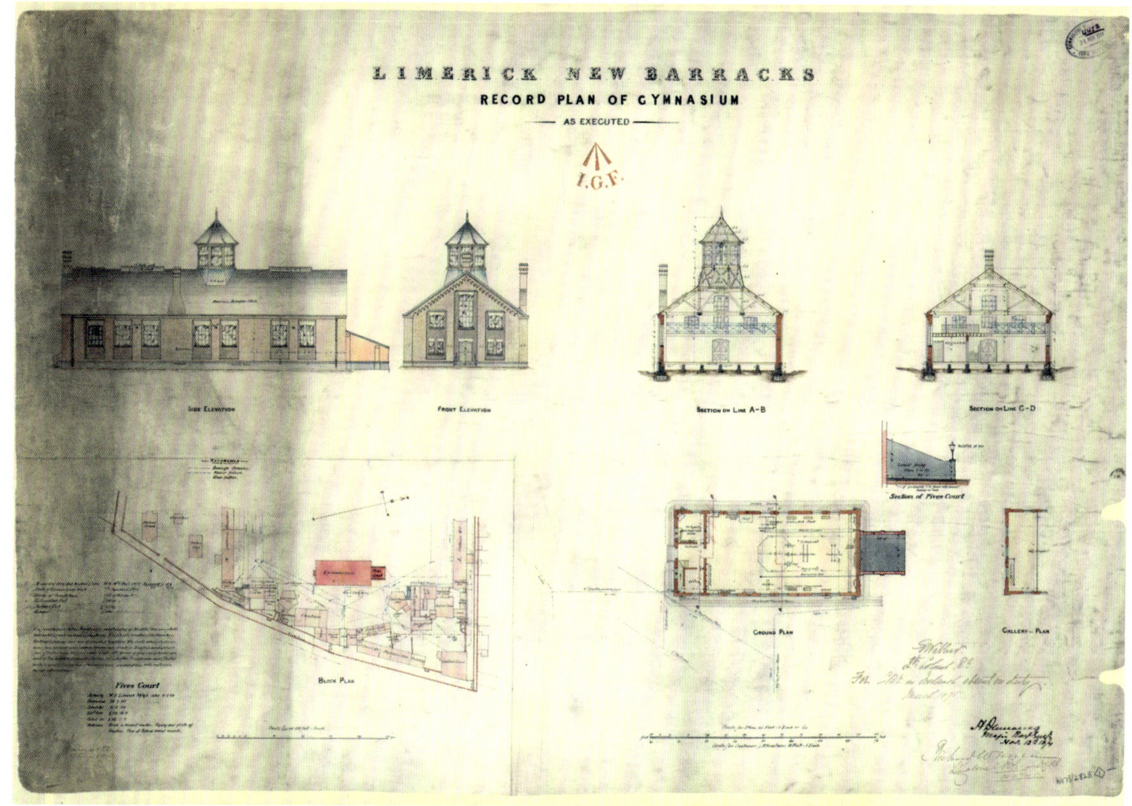

The officers of the Manchester Regiment in Limerick, 1894. (Courtesy of the Manchester Regiment Archives.)

The Manchester Regiment on the Square, 1894. (Courtesy of Manchester Regiment Archives.)

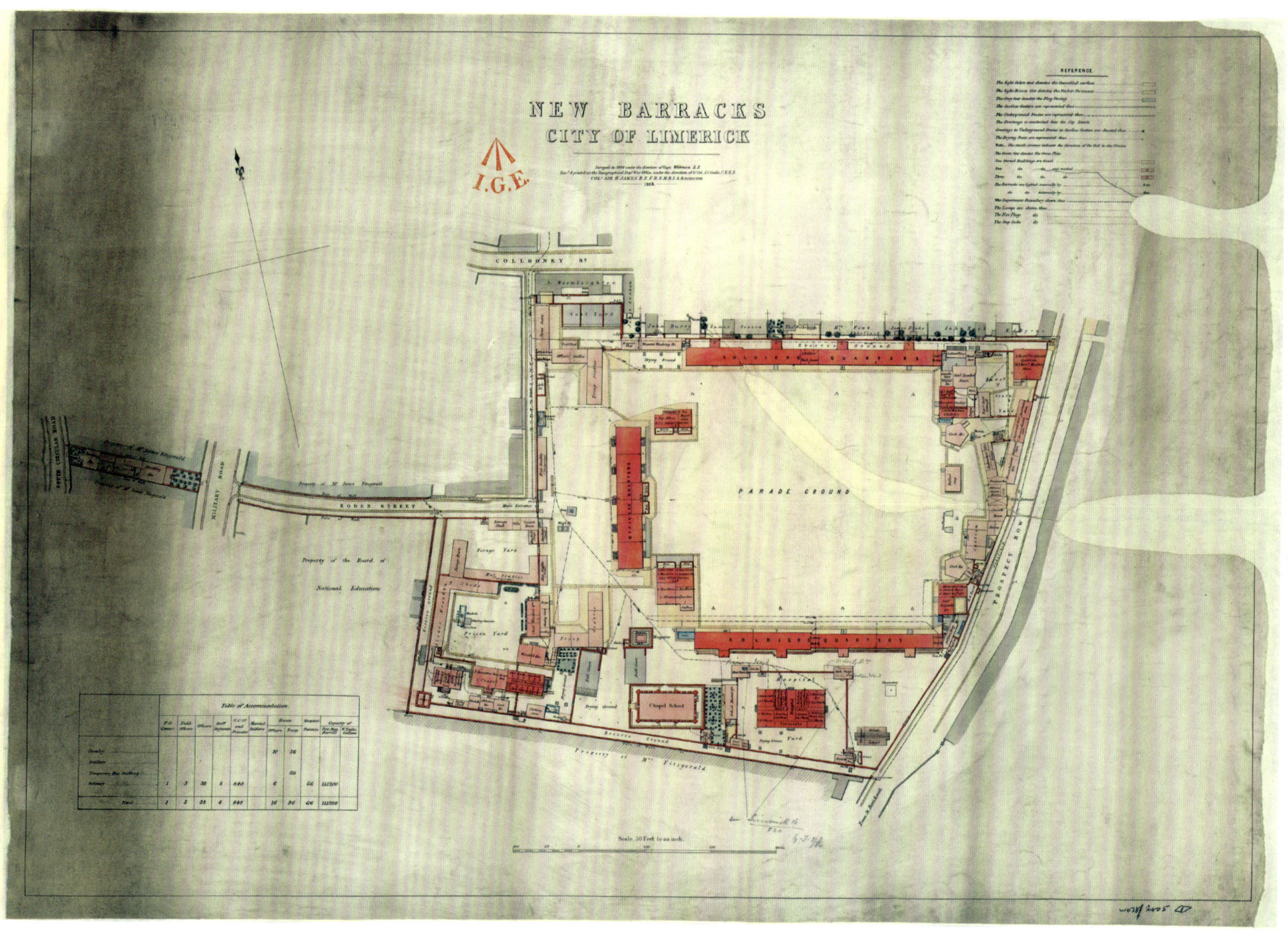

Map of New Barracks, Limerick, 1868.
(Courtesy of National Archives of United Kingdom.)

Left: Postcard of New Barracks, late nineteenth century.

Right: Postcard of New Barracks, late nineteenth century. (Courtesy of Limerick City Museum.)

Below: Nineteenth-century Barracks Parade. (Courtesy of the Lawrence Collection, N.C.I.)

Right: RAMC Medics in the Barracks Camp Field, 1915.
(Courtesy of RAMC Muniment Collection, Wellcome Library.)

Left: RAMC Medics on the Square, 1915.
(Courtesy of RAMC Muniment Collection, Wellcome Library.)

Right: RAMC Medics outside N Block, 1915.
(Courtesy of RAMC Muniment Collection, Wellcome Library.)

The tank 'Scotch and Soda' on the Barracks Camp Field, 1918.
(Courtesy of Limerick City Museum.)

RAMC on parade on the Square in 1915.
(Courtesy of Eagleston Brothers Photography.)

Above: First World War recruits in New Barracks. (Courtesy of Limerick Museum.)

Left: Military Parade on George's Street (O'Connell Street) in 1915. (Courtesy of RAMC Muniment Collection, Wellcome Library.)

Below: British Medics playing fives in the Barracks, 1915. (Courtesy of RAMC Muniment Collection, Wellcome Library.)

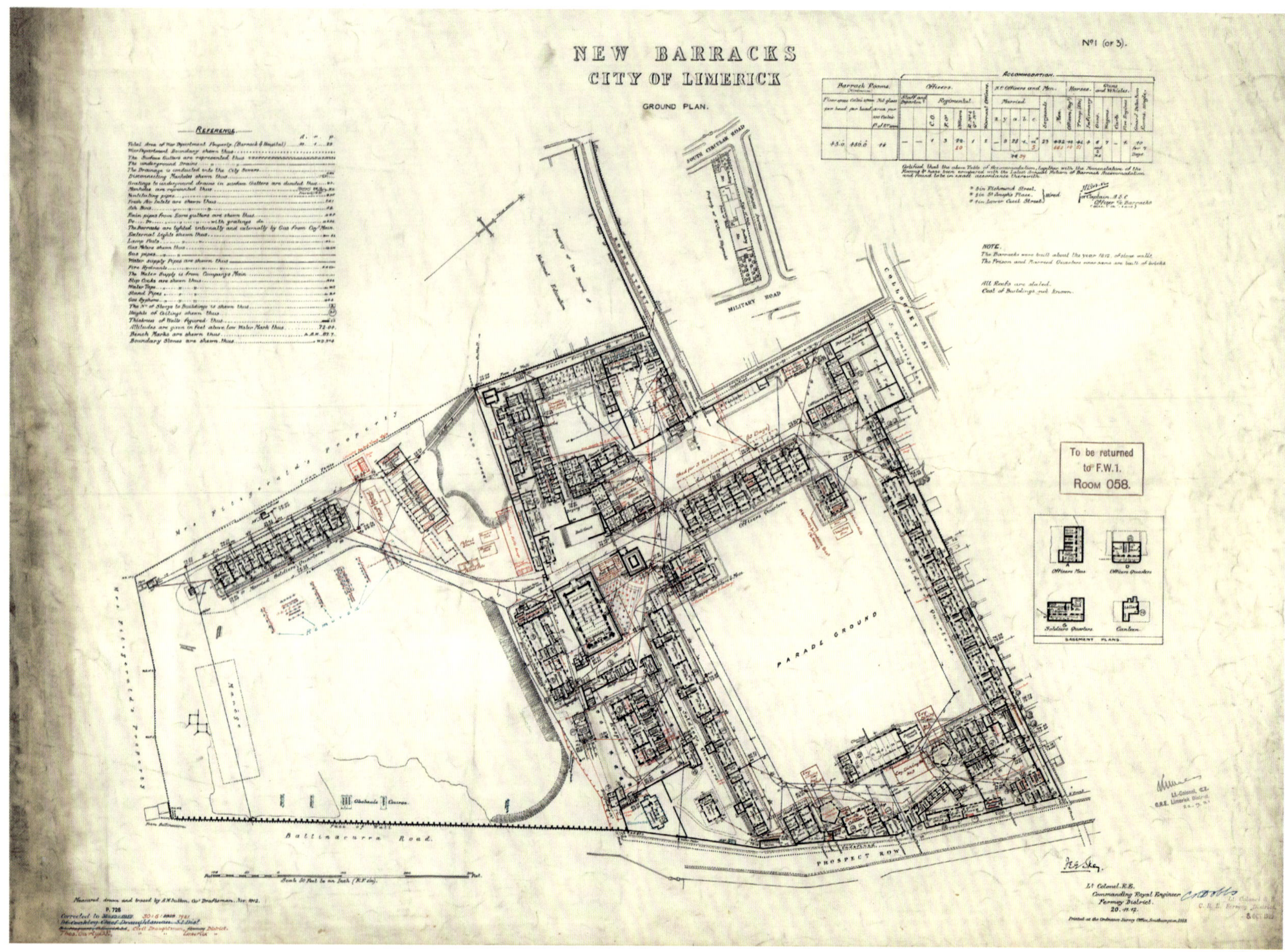

Map of New Barracks, 1912.
(Courtesy of National Archives of the United Kingdom.)

Chapter Two: From the War of Independence to the Emergency

With the end of the Great War and the 1916 Rising, Republicanism spread throughout Ireland. Between 1918 and 1922, mainly Scottish and Welsh Regiments manned the New Barracks. With the threat to the British Army posed by the growing number of Republican Forces, the British Government introduced a new force to Ireland, nicknamed locally as the Black and Tans because of their uniforms. This force was made up of ex-soldiers and police from Britain and had a brutal reputation. A number of these personnel were stationed in the New Barracks and various other locations in the city. It was during this period that the Barracks saw the introduction of new weaponry such as a First World War tank known as 'Scotch and Soda'. Crossley tenders, armoured cars and machine guns were also introduced to help the army in its policing role.

The Barracks Prison was used to hold IRA prisoners, Captain Thomas Keane being the most famous of these. He was the Company Commander, C Company, 2nd Battalion IRA. On 1 May 1921, Keane and another IRA member, Henry Clancy, were arrested by a joint RIC and Black and Tan patrol. Henry Clancy was shot dead while trying to escape; his body was taken to the morgue in the New Barracks. Captain Keane was held in Limerick Jail until his court martial, where he was sentenced to death by firing squad. On 3 June 1921, he was transferred to the Military Prison in the New Barracks, and executed the following day in the prison grounds. When a Free State was declared in 1922, the only official handover in Limerick took place in the Castle Barracks, where General Michael Brennan took command of the Castle Barracks from the Royal Welch Fusiliers. He later retreated from the City under pressure from superior Republican forces.

The New Barracks was vacated by the British in March 1922 and was looted by locals. IRA forces, under the command of General Liam Lynch, occupied the New Barracks, and the Barracks acted as the headquarters for the local IRA. However, under threat from Free State forces, the IRA evacuated the Barracks on 21 July 1922, burning it as they left. The Barracks then came under the command of Generals Brennan and Hannigan. The first unit of the Irish Army to occupy the Barracks was the 7th Infantry Battalion under the command of Commandant Liam Walsh. In March 1924, the Barracks housed the 4th Brigade of the Irish Army. By 1929, nearly all the buildings, with the exception of the Hospital, had been restored by Army Engineers, the Barracks then being home to part of the 4th Infantry Battalion under the command of Major Tommie Ryan. It was he who detailed a young Lieutenant called Sean Clancy to find a new name for the Barracks. New Barracks was renamed Sarsfield Barracks, after the famous Irish General, Patrick Sarsfield, in an official ceremony attended by local councillors and dignitaries. The Barracks was then blessed by the Barracks' Chaplain, Fr Dick McCarthy.

In 1934, the Thomond Regiment of the Irish Army was recruited from both Limerick and Clare and in 1935 a volunteer depot was set up under the command of Commandant Tom Crean. In 1939, the 9th Infantry Battalion were stationed in Sarsfield Barracks under the command of Lt-Col. Tom Halpin, possessing a strength of 700 officers and men.

The start of the Second World War led to a dramatic increase in the size of the army with the formation of a number of new Brigades. In Limerick, the 7th Brigade was established, with its headquarters in the Sarsfield Barracks, under the command of Colonel Tom Feeney. It was part of the 1st Division of the army, with divisional headquarters in Cork. During the War, Sarsfield Barracks was also home to the 7th Field Artillery Regiment, 7th Field Engineer Company, 7th Field Supply and Transport Company.

The establishment of the LDF saw the formation of a number of local defence units. The Barracks was used as a staging post for the vital jobs of protecting strategic installations and the training of Brigade units. During the Emergency the 7th Brigade became very efficient and achieved many sporting successes in rugby, hurling, and football.

In 1946, with the end of the Second World War, the army was reduced in size, resulting in the amalgamation of the 9th, 12th, 15th and 23rd Battalions into a new 12th Battalion. After a short spell in Knocknalisheen camp, the 12th Infantry Battalion moved to Sarsfield Barracks, where they have remained to this day. In 1946, the Reserve was reorganised and this led to the establishment of the 49th Infantry FCA Battalion in Sarsfield Barracks. At this time the main focus of the 12th Infantry Battalion was training and it achieved considerable success in shooting competitions and in sport. In 1946, the 12th Infantry Battalion won the honour of being named the Premier Battalion of the Army (Best Battalion), and was awarded a Pennant and Trophy, which is still held in the Officer's Mess, Sarsfield Barracks.

Captain Keane, executed in New Barracks, 1921.
(Courtesy of Limerick City Museum.)

IRA forces in New Barracks, 1922.

Right: The Barracks Hospital, burnt by the IRA in 1922.
(Courtesy of Limerick City Museum.)

Right: The Barracks church, burnt by the IRA in 1922.
(Courtesy of Limerick City Museum.)

Left: Accommodation Blocks burnt by the IRA in 1922.
(Courtesy of Limerick City Museum.)

58—THE ILLUSTRATED LONDON NEWS, July 29, 1922.

THE ILLUSTRATED LONDON NEWS, July 29, 1922.—

THE RELIEF OF LIMERICK: IRISH NATIONAL TROOPS CAPTURE THE CITY AFTER AN ARTILLERY ASSAULT.

Photographs by I.N.A. and Topical.

MOTORS, CARTS, AND SAND-BAGS AS BARRICADES: A MAIN-ROAD "BATTLEFRONT"—CRUISE'S ROYAL HOTEL ON THE RIGHT.

ONE OF MANY TRAPS SET BY THE IRREGULARS: A NATIONAL SOLDIER POINTING TO AN UNEXPLODED MINE IN A BARRACKS.

CONSTRUCTED FOR THE ATTACK ON AN IRREGULAR STRONGHOLD: THE SAND-BAGGED ENTRANCE, CRUISE'S HOTEL, BASEMENT.

PASSING THROUGH BARRICADES AT THE BRIDGEHEAD, LIMERICK: CHARS-A-BANCS WITH NATIONAL TROOPS FOR THE LIMERICK FIGHT.

WITH CIVILIANS MUCH INTERESTED IN THEM: NATIONAL TROOPS GUARDING A BREACH MADE BY THEIR SHELLS.

FRATERNISING WITH THE NATIONAL ARMY AFTER THE TAKING OF LIMERICK: PEOPLE OF THE LIBERATED CITY.

A RESULT OF SHELLS FIRED BY THE NATIONAL ARTILLERY: A BREACH IN THE BACK OF STRAND BARRACKS.

IRREGULAR DEFENCES: A BARRICADE IN A LIMERICK STREET.

USED BY THE IRREGULARS AND AFTERWARDS BURNT BY THEM: A LIMERICK CHURCH RUINED.

WITH CAPTAIN HANNON, ONE OF THE WOUNDED: A NATIONAL ARMY GROUP AFTER THE FIGHTING.

IRREGULAR DEFENCES: A BARRICADE IN A LIMERICK STREET.

The capture of Limerick by the National Army in 1922.
(Courtesy of Limerick City Museum.)

Right: The NCO's Mess burnt by the IRA in 1922.
(Courtesy of Limercik City Museum.)

Left: Private McInerney on sentry duty outside the main gate,
New Barracks, in the early 1920s.

Right: National Army in New Barracks in 1922.
(Courtesy of Limerick City Museum.)

Gen. Patrick Sarsfield, after whom the Barracks is named.
(Courtesy of Limerick City Museum.)

Col. Sean Clancy (Rtd), the officer who renamed the
Barracks at the grave of Captain Thomas Keane.

Officers of the 7th Brigade, Sarsfield Barracks, during the Emergency.

A group of Irish Army officers in Sarsfield Barracks, *c.*1930. (Courtesy of Eagleston Brothers Photography.)

Above: The funeral procession of Fr Chawke passing the location of the old Artillery Barracks on Mulgrave Street in 1948.

Below: Eucharistic Procession in Limerick, 1940s.

Above: The Mass card of Fr Chawke, the only Chaplain to die in service in Sarsfield Barracks.

Bren Gun Carrier on parade in Limerick, being reviewed by Taoiseach Eamonn de Valera, *c*. 1940.

The 12th Battalion gym team, 1949.

Chapter Three: From the 1950s to 1980s

In 1950, Sarsfield Barracks was under the command of Lieutenant Colonel J.P. Murphy, who was also the Commanding Officer of the 12th Infantry Battalion. The 12th Battalion, like other amalgamated units of the army had to adjust to its new status and became the core unit of Sarsfield Barracks. Military training remained the Barracks' primary role during the 1950s, with the battalion achieving considerable success in this role and winning many All-Army titles in shooting and sports. In December 1952, Lieutenant Colonel Murphy died in service, and was the only battalion Commander of the 12th Battalion to do so. The army was again restructured in 1959, resulting in the 13th Infantry Battalion (Kickham Barracks, Clonmel) being amalgamated into the 12th Infantry Battalion. Today, both B Company and the Support Company of the 12th Battalion remain in Clonmel.

The 1970s saw recruitment by the Defence Forces increase nationally, in response to the challenges faced by the State, both in Ireland and overseas. For Sarsfield Barracks, this led to the creation of a new company – C Company of the 12th Battalion. However, in 1985, C Company, 12th Infantry Battalion was stood down due to restructuring within the Defence Forces. The 1980s saw the intake of recruits for the army slowing down with the economic state of the country in decline. However, the 1980s did create a little piece of battalion history. In 1986, after many years of losing numerous finals and semi-finals, the 12th Battalion won the Cunningham Cup, the All-Army soccer competition. This was followed by a second cup victory in 1988.

During the 1960s, troops from Sarsfield Barracks began overseas service in places such as the Congo and Cyprus. However, 1969 saw trouble flare up in Northern Ireland, and this brought about the deployment of troops from Sarsfield Barracks for duty on the Border. The 1970s saw a sharp rise in operational commitments due to the threat caused by the Troubles in the North, with troops performing security duties in the Silvermines (1971–1986), Money Point power station (1970–1980) and Alcan Aluminium Plant (1978-1981). In 1974, troops from Sarsfield Barracks also commenced additional security duties in Limerick Prison. Outside of these security duties, troops were used in the role of aid to the civil power on several occasions, for instance, during the petrol strike, the fire strike, the bin strike, the bus strike and the prison officer strikes of the 1970s and 1980s. It was not only overseas that members of the 12th Battalion were to provide assistance to refugees; in 1957-58, Knockalisheen camp became a refugee camp for Hungarian refugees and Sarsfield Barracks was assigned full responsibility for the camp during this period.

Ceremonial duties were also important, and the 12th Battalion was to provide some high-profile guards of honour during this period, notably for President De Valera in 1961, President John F. Kennedy in 1963, President Tito in 1978, Pope John Paul II in 1979, President Regan in 1984, and King Juan Carlos of Spain in 1986.

Left: 12th Battalion, Combined Weapons Cup Winners, 1950s.

Right: 12th Battalion, Bren Gun Cup Winners, 1950s.

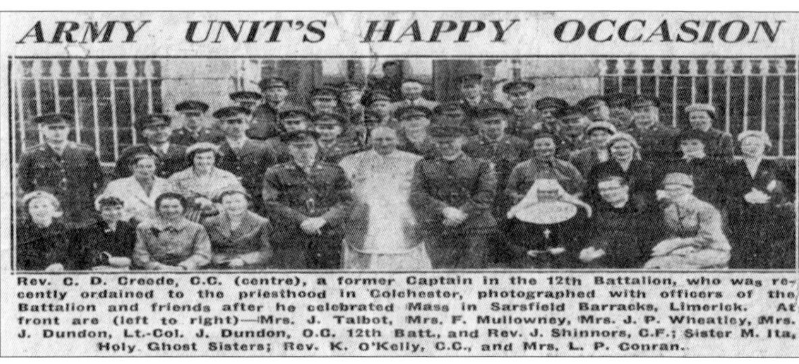

Rev. C. D. Creede, C.C. (centre), a former Captain in the 12th Battalion, who was recently ordained to the priesthood in Colchester, photographed with officers of the Battalion and friends after he celebrated Mass in Sarsfield Barracks, Limerick. At front are (left to right)—Mrs. J. Talbot, Mrs. F. Mullowney, Mrs. J. P. Wheatley, Mrs. J. Dundon, Lt.-Col. J. Dundon, O.C. 12th Batt., and Rev. J. Shinnors, C.F.; Sister M. Ita, Holy Ghost Sisters; Rev. K. O'Kelly, C.C., and Mrs. L. P. Conran.

Left: The 1953 Recruit Platoon, Sarsfield Barracks.

Right: A newspaper cutting of the Ordination of Captain Creede, 1957. The accompanying article read:
'Revd C.D. Creede CC, who was recently ordained in Colchester, England, celebrated Mass in the Garrison church, Sarsfield Barracks, Limerick, where he had formerly served for three years as a captain. A native of Tullow, he retired from the army six years ago to study for the priesthood. It was on the invitation of Lt-Col. J. Dundon, OC 12th Battalion, that he visited the Barracks to celebrate the Mass, which was attended by many of his former brother officers, NCOs, and men of the 12th Battalion and their wives. The was a guard of honour and full military honours were accorded at the Elevation. Subsequently Fr Creede was presented with an address of welcome by Lt-Col. Dundon, who paid tribute to his many sterling qualities. The newly ordained priest will minister in the Diocese of Brentford, Brentwood. The attendance included Revd K. O'Kelly CC, a native of Sixmilebridge, Co. Clare, who was also recently ordained in England.'

Above: A public parade by the 12th Battalion on the streets of Limerick in 1958.

Left: Private Jimmy Sullivan, 12th Battalion, *c*.1958.

Below: Private Patrick Touhy receiving his service medal in Sarsfield Barracks, 1950s.

The Southern Command Boxing Team in Sarsfield Barracks, 1960s.

Left: The former Chief of Staff Gen. Sean McKeown as a Major in Sarsfield Barracks.

Right: Lt-Col. Dundon, OC Sarsfield Barracks, 1950s.

Below: Christmas dinner in the Barracks, with the officers serving the men, 1960s.

12th Battalion Mortar Team, All-Army Champions, 1966.

Sergeant Major Bill Dollard, 1970s.

Guard of Honour for De Valera, 1959.

Honour Guard for two Colonels in Sarsfield Barracks, early 1970s.

12th Battalion Team, Cunningham Team, early 1980s.

On exercise in the 1970s.

Mayoress Condell in the Barracks in 1970s.

Guard of Honour for King Juan Carlos of Spain, 1986.

Right: 12th Battalion Recruit Platoon, 1981.

Below: 12th Battalion at Kilworth, 1981

Left: Guard of Honour for Pope John Paul II at Shannon Airport, 1979.

Right: Guard of Honour for Tito, President of Yugoslavia, 1978.

Left: Classroom instruction for support weapons, early 1980s.

A Battalion Parade in Sarsfield Barracks, 1980s.

Chapter Four: The Modern Barracks

The modern era has seen troops from Sarsfield Barracks continue the tradition of service to the State, and though 1991 saw the withdrawal of troops from Limerick Prison, the 12th Battalion began security duties at Portlaoise Prison on a rotational basis, while Cash Escorts have also become a routine part of Barracks life. One of the biggest challenges experienced was in 2004, when Sarsfield Barracks played its part in one of the biggest operational movements of troops in the history of the State – Operation Munster Summit. The battalion continues to be tasked with the provision of honour guards for visiting foreign dignities; these ceremonial commitments have included the visit of the King and Queen of Norway amongst others.

In the early 1990s, many physical changes were made within the Barracks, including the development of a new entrance, the opening of a new NCO Mess and the improvement of many buildings within the Barracks with the replacement of windows and roofs. It was during the late 1990s that married quarters came to an end, as most soldiers no longer lived within the confines of the Barracks. Barrack refurbishment was continued in the early part of 2000, and by 2005, the second phase in the refurbishment of the blocks had been completed. In 2006, P Block was renovated and 2008 saw the opening of a new dining hall and Privates' Mess. The Gym Building will also be refurbished by 2009.

1989 saw the introduction of the Steyr Rifle, a weapon the 12th Battalion quickly mastered; in the first All-Army rifle competition with rifle, the 12th Battalion were victorious. In 1990, the 12th Battalion won the Southern Command shooting competition and it has continued to enjoy success in shooting competitions, winning a number of All-Army titles. One of the 12th Battalion's finest hours came in 1995, when the battalion won the All-Army Falling Plates competition, going on to win the first International Falling Plates competition on the same day. The battalion has achieved success in more than just shooting competitions; in 2006 the 12th Battalion scored a major success in winning the Chaplain's Cup in hurling.

In 1991, two soldiers from Sarsfield Barracks were given one of Ireland's highest military honours, when Privates Edward Long and Richard Penny were each awarded the Distinguished Service Medal. Privates Long and Penny risked their lives while on duty at Fenit Pier, Co. Kerry, in the rescue of a drowning sailor in the harbour in difficult weather conditions.

The 1990s also saw another reorganisation of the Defence Forces. Although the structure of the 12th Battalion was not altered, this reorganisation abolished the old Southern Command structure and the 12th Battalion became part of 1st Southern Brigade. There was also the introduction of a voluntary early redundancy scheme, which saw Sarsfield Barracks lose a number of its longest serving personnel. Today, the role of the soldiers of Sarsfield Barracks remains almost as it was from the foundation of the State, with the majority of a soldier's time being spent in Barrack duties, aid to the civil power and training, while overseas, new challenges have been created for the Irish soldier.

Above left: An Alouette III takes off in Sarsfield Barracks.

Above right: A night-time exercise in the Barracks, 1985.

Below: An aerial view of Sarsfield Barracks.

The 12th Battalion at Rockhill, Co. Donegal, during Operation Mallard, 1987.

Left: 12th Battalion platoon on Border operations, 1987.

Below: The 12th Battalion *en route* to Operation Mallard, 1987.

Right: The 12th Battalion win the International Falling Plate Competition at Curragh in 1995. (Courtesy of *The Star*.)

OUR LADS SHOOT UP TO THE TOP

By MARK McGUINNESS

IRELAND'S riflemen are among the best in the world - and that's official!

The eagle-eyed troops shot the world's top marksmen out of the water. In warlike conditions they beat the best of British, American and Finnish shooters.

This latest flash of Irish pride was triggered at the International Falling Plates Competition at the Curragh last Wednesday.

It was all part of the celebrations of the United Nations 50th anniversary.

The rules of the competition made it all the more difficult for the riflemen to get their shots on target.

Each team contained six marksmen. As soon as a whistle was blown they had to run 25 metres, dive to the ground and shoot at 10 plates (each one a foot long and wide) placed 200 metres away.

This is hard enough on its own. But the teams were competing against each other - running side by side - trying to get the shots off and plates down quicker than the team beside them.

Pressure

An Army spokesman said: "This is more difficult than simple shooting - it's a test of speed and aim under pressure.

"This is the kind of shooting you would be doing if you were in a war situation."

The first shoot-out was between the Finnish Battalion (Finnbatt) and the E Company 51st Battalion (American), and was the best of three. The Finns won.

The British sent the best they had - the deadly efficient 3rd Battalion Royal Gurkha Rifles.

The battle hardened legion which lead Britain to victory in the Falklands War, arrived armed with the best of rifles - complete with high accuracy telescopic sights on top.

But they hadn't reckoned on the fighting spirit of the Irish 12th Battalion, based in Limerick.

It was a close call. The determind Limerickmen needed only two runs to beat the old enemy - And they did it.

This left the 77th Battalion - who flew home from Lebanon for the competition - to bring up the second flank. They easily saw off the Finns in the semi-final.

Lebanon

This set up an all-Irish final between the Limerickmen and the 77th battalion.

The 12th battalion came out on top in the first two competitions - and were crowned champions.

ON TARGET: The 12th Limerick Battalion

OME FROM THE FRONT: The 77th Battalion

IN LINE: Lt Gen Gerry McMahon meets the Gurk

Left: A boxing match in the gym at Sarsfield Barracks, 1980s.

Right: The 12th Battalion win the All-Army Falling Plate Competition at Curragh in 1993. (Courtesy of *The Irish Times*.)

Stand-down parade for Sergeant Major Dermot O'Keeffee, 2007.

Stand-down parade for Sergeant Major Cyril Shanahan.

Right and below: 12th
Battalion on parade, 2003.

Left: Corporals Carroll and Nugent receive their state stripes from Gen. O'Callaghan, GOC 1st Southern Brigade, 2006.

Right: The O'Neill family – three generations of service with the 12th Battalion.

12th Battalion 112th Recruit Platoon, 2005.

Above: President McAleese inspects a 12th Battalion Guard of Honour, June 2000.

Left: President McAleese meets the oldest and youngest soldiers in Sarsfield Barracks, June 2000.

Below: President McAleese and the Officers of Sarsfield Barracks, June 2000.

12th Battalion 112th Recruit Platoon, 2005,
Privates McEllroy, O'Hanlon, and Leahy.

A MOWAG convoy *en route* to Shannon
Airport, 2005. (Courtesy of *The Irish Times*.)

Above, left and right: Preparation for the Munster Summit, 2005.

Below: A winter morning in Sarsfield Barracks, 2007.

Left: The laying of the foundation stone for the new dining hall and Privates' Mess by the Minister of Defence, Mr Willie O'Dea, 2005.

Right: The opening of the new dining hall and Privates' Mess by the Minister of Defence, Mr Willie O'Dea, 2006.

Left: The catering staff, 12th Battalion, at the opening of the new dining hall and Privates' Mess, 2006.

IUNVA Chairman William Keane and Lt-Col. Michael Shannon (Rtd), at the opening of the new dining hall and Privates' Mess, 2006.

Three services at the opening of the new dining hall and Privates' Mess, 2006. Chief Superintendent William Keane, Lt-Col. Tony Daly, and Civil Defence Officer Josh Kirby.

The opening shot at the JP MacManus Golf Classic, Adare, Co. Limerick, 2005.

The 12th Battalion Soccer Team, Cunningham Cup Winners, 1988.

George Foreman visits Sarsfield Barracks, 1999.

The 12th Battalion Hurling Team, Chaplain's Cup Winners, 2006.

The 12th Battalion and PDF Cadre on parade, 2008.

Above: 12th Battalion Pipe Band, 1992.

Right: Retirement of Captain Michael Egan.

Below: 12th Battalion Pipe Band on parade, St Patrick's Day, Limerick.

Brigadier-General Pat Nash inspects the PDF Cadre Staff of the FCA, 2004.

The New NCOs receive their stripes from Lt-Col. Carroll, 2008.

Glenn Hughes, now sadly deceased, is shown some of the Army's weapons by Sergeant Gerry Barry on a visit to Sarsfield Barracks with his friends 2007.

The Chaplains of Sarsfield Barracks.

Above left: Members of Sarsfield Barracks on parade, 2008.

Above right: Battalion Sergeant Major Dinnen and Battalion Quartermaster Sergeant McNamara.

Below: The Opening of Sarsfield Barracks' Museum, by Brigadier-General Pat Nash and Lt-Col. Michael McMahon, 2004.

123rd Recruit Platoon, 2008.

Chapter Five: The Barracks and Overseas Service

While many British regiments left the then New Barracks to serve overseas, the first soldiers from the 12th Battalion left Ireland in 1960 for service in the Congo. This was to be the start of over fifty years of international peacekeeping service by the men and women of the 12th Battalion and other soldiers based at Sarsfield Barracks. The Congo was a dangerous and challenging mission and one which contributed greatly to the development of the Defence Forces in the late twentieth century.

Cyprus was to be the next challenge for the 12th Battalion and other units, with a UN mission being established there in 1964 after the Turkish invasion of Northern Cyprus. When stationed in Cyprus, troops from the 25th Infantry Group were moved to the Sinai from 1973 to 1974 in order to stabilise the situation after the Yom Kippur War. The Northern Troubles limited overseas deployment of Irish troops until 1978, when the Irish Government agreed to send soldiers to Lebanon after the Israeli invasion. This was to become Ireland's longest commitment to a single mission, with an Irish battalion remaining in Lebanon until 2001. Two soldiers from Sarsfield Barracks, Sergeant John Power and Private Michael Dillon were awarded the Distinguished Service Medal in 1980, during their tours, for outstanding courage in the defence of their posts and their fellow soldiers. Soldiers from the 12th Battalion returned to Lebanon in 2006, after another Israeli invasion in that year.

Soldiers from Sarsfield Barracks have served all over the world on UN and European missions, serving in Somalia from 1993 to 1995 with UNOSOM II. Troops have also served in the Balkans, from 1997 to the present day, providing assistance to the Regional Governments with SFOR and later EUFOR missions. Since 1999, the 12th Battalion has been lead-battalion twice for the PfP mission in Kosovo, as part of a stabilisation mission after the withdrawal of Serbian Forces. Irish servicemen were part of UNMEE from 2000 to 2003, keeping the peace in Ethiopia and Eritrea. At the same time, soldiers from the 12th Battalion were also in East Timor as part of the Irish Government's commitment to assisting the new state's transition to independence. Ireland's commitment to international peace and the protection of vulnerable global communities continues with the EUFOR CHAD mission.

Since 1960, the men and women of Sarsfield Barracks have shown themselves to be dedicated to overseas service and the professionalism it requires. They have operated in all corners of the world, in all climates and environments, and maintained the highest personal and military standards in so doing. As long as Ireland continues to send peacekeepers overseas, one thing is certain – that the servicemen and women of Sarsfield Barracks will always play a prominent role and continue to do their Barracks proud.

The first contingent from Sarsfield Barracks to leave for the Congo, 1960. Back row: Pte. Lacey, Pte. (Balikie) Paddy O'Connor, 63 Lenihan Avenue, Prospect (who kindly supplied the three pictures), Pte. Kevin Hayes, Pte. Kevin Hickey, ——, ——, Pte. O'Dea, Pte. Gay Reddan, Pte. P. Morgan, Pte. M. Whelan (R.I.P.). Second row: Pte. Dave Hayes, ——, ——, ——, ——, ——, ——, Pte. Tony Moylan, ——, Pte. John McCormack, Pte. Billy Kane. Front row: ——, ——, Sgt. Jim Enright, Cllr. Paddy Kelly, Mayor, who gave the troops a civic send off; ——, Sgt. Mick O'Leary, ——, Sergt. Danny Cotter (R.I.P.).

Above left: Prayers prior to departure for the Congo, 1960.

Above right: 12th Battalion Soldiers leaving for the Congo, 1961.

Left: A newspaper cutting of the first Limerick soldiers leaving for service in the Congo, 1960.

12th Battalion Soldiers return from the Congo, 1961.

Left: 12th Battalion Band in Cyprus, 1967.

Right: 12th Battalion Band in Cyprus, 1967.

Left: Corporal Eamonn O'Riordan on patrol in Cyprus, 1972.

Corporal Barney Ryan on fitter duty in Cyprus, 1972.

12th Battalion personnel in the Sinai Desert, 1974.

12th Battalion in Lebanon, 1978.

December in Lebanon, 1985.

Above: Sarsfield Barracks personnel in Lebanon.

Left: Establishing Comms in the Lebanon.

Below: Christmas in Lebanon.

Private Sean Gleeson in Somalia with members of the Indian Army.

Members of 12th Battalion with other Irish Soldiers and Somali refugees.

Members of 12th Battalion returning from patrol in East Timor, 2000.

On jungle patrol in East Timor, 2000.

UN helicopter collecting 12th Battalion patrol in East Timor jungle, 2000.

Hearts and Minds in East Timor, 2000.

Above: Kosovo Mission, 2005, Sarsfield Barracks.

Below: Members of 12th Battalion on parade prior to departure for Kosovo, 2007.

Above: Sergeant Tommy Boyce and his son Private Jason Boyce with Minister Willie O'Dea, prior to their departure for Kosovo 2007.

Below: Minister for Defence, Mr Willie O'Dea with members of Sarsfield Barracks who prepare to depart for Kosovo, 2007.

Left: Corporal Bridget Ahern prior to her departure for Kosovo, 2007.

Below: No. 2 Transport Coy, Kosovo, 2000.

Right: A MOWAG APC overlooks the city of Pristina.

Below: An Irish sniper team in Kosovo.

Private Quinlivan establishing satellite communications in Eritrea.

Soldiers from the 12th Battalion on the UNMEE mission.

Teresa Davidson accompanies members of the 12th Battalion on patrol in At-tiri village, South Lebanon, 1992.

Left: ONE/IUNVA Veterans Parade in Sarsfield Barracks on UN Day.

Right: UN Day, 2005.

Left: Wreath-laying ceremony, UN Day, 2005.

Chapter Six: The Reserves

Reserves have been an integral part of the life of Sarsfield Barracks since the 1920s. A Class 'A' Reserve was formed in 1927, comprised of ex-Regulars transferred to reserve service. The existence of this reserve allowed the army to expand rapidly in 1939, when faced with the threat of the Second World War, known in Ireland as 'the Emergency'.

A Class 'B' Reserve created at the same time never really developed, and was replaced in 1934, by the then Fianna Fáil Government with a Volunteer Force. This new reserve was designed to attract former Anti-Treaty supporters into the army. As part of this new reserve, the Thomond Regiment was established in Limerick and Clare. This Volunteer Force was distinguished from the Regulars by a darker uniform and different insignia.

The Emergency brought new military and security challenges for the Irish Government and the Volunteer Force, many of whom were now called to active service. A Garda Act in 1940 created a Local Security Force, which was subdivided into an 'A' Group and a 'B' Group. The 'B' Group was assigned as an auxiliary to the Garda Síochána. The 'A' Group became the Local Defence Force, or to give its Irish name, An Fórsa Cosanata Áitúil (FCA). This was predominantly an infantry force.

In 1947, the Reserves were reorganised, with the FCA becoming the 2nd Line Reserve. In 1959, the concept of 'integration' was introduced, with six mixed brigades of both full-time and reserve personnel being created. This changed again in 1979, with four full-time brigades being created and the formation of a Directorate of Reserve Forces. In 1997, A Slua Muirí (Naval Reserve Company) was formed in Sarsfield Barracks.

1959 saw the disbandment of the 49th Battalion, which had been based in Sarsfield Barracks. Some of its personnel were reorganised into reserve support units which were to remain in the Barracks until 2005. The 3rd Field Engineers were formed from the pioneer platoon of the 49th, while other members of the 49th became the 3rd Anti-Aircraft Battery. The 3rd Field Signals and Transport Companies were also formed in 1959. Other units were to follow; the 3rd Field Military Police Company being formed in 1961, and the 3rd Field Medical Company in 1964.

In 2005 a new Reserve Defence Force was launched, reflecting the structure of the existing regular brigades. For the reserve community in Sarsfield Barracks, this meant several changes. The 14th Battalion from Sarsfield Barracks has merged with the 22nd Battalion from Clare and the 15th Battalion from Kerry to become part of the new 32nd Infantry Battalion. The 3rd Field Military Police has merged with the former 1st Field Military Police of Cork to create the new 31st Reserve Military Police Company, while the 3rd Field Supply and Transport Company merged with the 3rd Field Medical Company to form the 31st Reserve Logistical Support Battalion. The 3rd Field Signal Company was renamed the 31st Reserve Communications and Information Systems Company. This change has signalled a new direction for the Reserve. Integration has given reservists the chance to train alongside their regular counterparts, and the opportunity of United Nation's service is imminent. In short, service in the various reserve units of Sarsfield Barracks is growing more and more demanding and challenging as it enters the twenty-first century.

Left: The 49th Battalion on exercise in the 1940s.

Right: The Commanding Officer of the 3rd Field Signals swears in a new recruit, 1950s.

Left: Classroom instruction, 3rd Field Signals, 1950s.

Right: Instruction in the Gustav submachine gun in the 1960s.

Left: 3rd Field Military Police and Motorcycles, 1950s.

Right: An MP Inspection Parade in Sarsfield Barracks in the 1960s.

First Reserve Female Recruit Platoon on the Range, 1980s.

3rd Field Military Police Company in their HQ at Sarsfield Barracks in the 1980s.

First Reserve Female Recruit Platoon in Sarsfield Barracks, 1980s.

Sergeant Kelly of the 14th Battalion gives a class in the Steyr Rifle in Sarsfield Barracks in early 2000.

Above: Lieutenant Kelly of the 14th Battalion and of the 32nd Battalion of the new Army Reserve, folds the old FCA standard on the Square of Sarsfield Barracks, 2005.

Below: The new integrated RDF Platoon of the 12th Battalion at Sarsfield Barracks, 2005.

The new integrated RDF Platoon of the 12th Battalion on the Range, 2005.

Lieutenant Denis O'Connell, RDF, gives orders to his platoon on tactics, 2005.

The new integrated RDF Platoon practise helicopter drills at Sarsfield Barracks, 2007.

The Naval Reserve on parade on St Patrick's Day in Sarsfield Barracks, 2007.

31 Reserve Military Police Class from a methods of instruction course held October 2007.

Right: Senior NCOs of 31 MP carry the relic of St Thérèse of Lisieux in Limerick, 2001.

Left: Members of 31 Engineers on adventure training.

Right: A Bofors EI-70 of the 3rd Air Defence Battery in action.

Appendix One: Boxing in Sarsfield Barracks

The 12th Infantry Battalion has always had a very strong boxing tradition, dating back to the 1940s and 1950s when it was at its strongest. Many All-Army titles made their way to Limerick, thanks to boxers such as Paddy McInerney and Timmors McCarthy, to name just two. Paddy joined the army in 1956 as the reigning Munster Champion and won an All-Army title that same year. He was coached by Bill Logan of St Francis Boxing Club, and was one of the great flyweights of his era.

Another boxing great was Timmors McCarthy who boxed as a flyweight and bantamweight, winning two All-Army titles as well as the Munster and Irish titles. He also competed for Ireland against Wales and Germany. It is no surprise that Timmors was such a skilful boxer, having lived across the road from St Francis Boxing Club of which he was a member. Timmors loved his training and it showed in the ring. His sons followed in his footsteps by joining the army and boxing with success.

These are just two of many fighters that have represented the 12th Battalion and Sarsfield Barracks. Others that did so are Mucks Ryan, the O'Donnell brothers, Harry Naughton and Christy Kelly. Christy later boxed as a professional and had a great record to boot. In the mid-1970s, the DeLoughrey brothers, Tony, Jerome and Pat, won five titles between them, before being barred from boxing in the army as they were classed as Senior Boxers. Tony and Jerome won many caps for their country.

In the 1990s came Pat O'Halloran, another flyweight, who did the 12th Battalion and Sarsfield Barracks proud, winning All-Army and Irish titles on the way to representing his country at international level.

This is just a glimpse of boxing in the 12th Battalion. There are many more who could have been mentioned if space allowed. Boxing today is no longer as popular as it once was in the army and there are no more army championships, but the 12th Battalion can look back on its boxing history with pride.

Yours in Sport,
Tony Deloughrey

Appendix Two: Chaplaincy – Sarsfield Barracks

In my short time as Chaplain with the Irish Defence Forces I have yet to meet another Chaplain, past or present, who has not enjoyed their time with the army. It certainly is a 'life less ordinary' and one that I would never have envisaged for myself. It is a great privilege to be of service to the Defence Forces.

Chaplains have served the personnel at Sarsfield Barracks for the past ninety years. From 1918 to 1942 the local clergy of St Michael's parish served as Chaplains. Then in 1942, the first official full-time Chaplain was appointed. His name was Fr John Chawke. What is interesting here from a personal point of view, and why I feel delighted to be asked to contribute this article, is because Fr Chawke was a first cousin of my late grandfather James Storin.

Fr John Chawke was Chaplain of Sarsfield Barracks until his death at the young age of thirty-nine on 12 January 1948.

Chaplains of Sarsfield Barracks

Revd James Hayes	1918	RIP, 1948.
Revd Maurice Fitzpatrick	1921	RIP, 13 May 1940.
Revd Edmond R. McCarthy	1921	RIP, 3 October 1964.
Revd Charles Moriarty	1933	RIP, 12 January 1965.
Revd John White	1937	RIP, 25 March 1974.
Revd Robert O'Sullivan	1939	RIP, 30 September 1965.
Revd John Chawke	September 1941 – 12 January 1948,	
RIP, 12 January 1948.		
Revd Joseph Shinnors	1 March 1948 – 26 April 1962,	
RIP, 7 April 1997.		
Revd Sean Condon	21 June 1962 – 4 July 1967,	
USA & St John's.		
Revd Sean Murphy	12 October 1967 – 31 October 1969,	
RIP, 10 January 1998.		
Revd Frank Moriarty	1 November 1969 – 11 February 1978,	
Retired PP, Adare.		
Revd Joseph Dempsey	12 February 1978 – 31 August 1985,	
PP, Rathkeale.		
Revd Desmond Campion	1 September 1985 – 30 June 1987,	
Navy Chaplain.		
Revd John O' Shea	1 July 1987 – 30 November 1992,	
PP, Abbeyfeale.		
Revd William Walsh	1 December 1992 – 30 November 2006, PP, Holy Rosary,	
Revd Seamus Madigan	1 December 2006 to date,	

Thanks to Fr Willie Walsh, a new plaque in the church records the names of the Chaplains who served in Sarsfield Barracks since 1918.

Overseas Service

Over the past forty-five years, Chaplains from this Barracks have accompanied army personnel in peacekeeping missions abroad. Fr Joseph Shinnors (1948–1962) was one of the first Irish Chaplains to go on an overseas mission, travelling to the Congo. Fr Sean Condon also did a tour of duty in the Congo.

Fr Frank Moriarty served overseas in Cyprus and Fr Joe Dempsey served in Lebanon. Fr John O' Shea did two tours of duty in the Lebanon, as did Fr Willie Walsh. Fr Willie Walsh also served in Liberia and Kosovo. And, as I write this article I am preparing from my first tour of duty to Kosovo!

Thanks

Have you got a minute Father?

The Chaplains of Sarsfield Barracks have gladly given of their time to the army here in Limerick, overseas, and more recently in Kickham Barracks, Clonmel. Each has brought their own giftedness to their ministry and I believe all of them have many happy memories of this place. You only have to listen to them tell stories of their time here!

It is a wonderful privilege and honour to serve as Chaplain to the Defence Forces. It's a most unique ministry for us Priests. I describe it as a great adventure. You never know what tomorrow brings, and each day, each moment in fact, brings its own blessings thanks to you, the serving and retired members of the Forces and your families. On my own behalf and of the Chaplains that have gone before me, I would like to express a very big thank you for all the support that has been given to the Padres over the past ninety years at Sarsfield Barracks.

Míle Buíochas! (A thousand thanks!)
Seamus Madigan

Appendix Three: The Charter of Sarsfield Barracks/New Barracks 1795-1798

Of the ground rented for the purposes of this Barracks, a space twenty feet broad parallel to the rear wall of the private buildings has been left outside the said wall along the entire of the SW flank line of building next John the Thos Monsell Esq. rs Ground and a space eight feet broad parallel to the rear wall of Privates buildings has been left outside the said wall along the entire of the NE D'estre Esq. rs as passages and a space of two feet parallel to the NW rear wall of the stables to which the back gate piers are attached has been left outside said rear wall to preclude any future claim whatsoever to a right of building against the said wall. The Building commenced and one range of Officers Building. Five Houses for Privates the Infirmary the Guard house Gateway and Prisons the Barracks Master store the Military store Ten double stables for the Calvary. One Stable for the infantry Officers Two Forges and Shoeing Shed the Coal yard the Surrounding wall and circular Enclosing walls were finished.

Garham Myers Esq. Arch
John Giblon, Contractor

Appendix Four: Captain Thomas Keane

Captain Thomas Keane was the most famous of the IRA prisoners held in the New Barracks during the War of Independence. Prior to his death he had been promoted to the rank of Captain, holding the post of Company Commander, C Company 2nd Battalion, IRA. He was married with two children and lived in Moors Lane, Limerick. On 1 May 1921, after picking up weapons, Keane and another IRA member, Henry Clancy, were arrested in a field just beyond Shanavaugha bridge. They were arrested by a joint RIC and Auxiliary Patrol. Sergeant Horan, a notorious officer, was in charge of the patrol.

Events leading to their arrests are not fully certain as official newspaper reports show that witnesses at Captain Keane's court martial, stated he fired at least one shot at the patrol. History books written on the period state he had no ammunition and was only collecting the weapons at the time. However, it is known that they were arrested, and Clancy, who was well known to his captors, tried to escape and was shot dead. His body was taken to the morgue in the New Barracks in Limerick.

Capt. Keane was held in Limerick Jail until his trial on 14 May 1921 where he was charged with two offences; levying war against His Majesty the King and being improperly in possession of a revolver. Keane was found guilty and sentenced to death – execution by firing squad. On 3 June 1921 at 10.00a.m., Keane was transferred from Limerick Jail to the Military Prison in the New Barracks. His wife and mother visited him that night and the next morning at 7.00a.m. he celebrated Mass in his cell with Fr Hayes.

Shortly after 8.00a.m. Captain Keane was taken to the prison courtyard and executed by firing squad. At the time of his execution, large crowds gathered outside on the roadway at the Redemptorist church to pray for him, the crowd being prevented from gathering at the Barracks gate by order of the courts. It is reported that this crowd of people was attacked by the Black and Tans in an attempt to disperse the crowds. Captain Keane's body was buried in the grounds of Limerick Jail and later exhumed and buried in the Republican plot in Mount St Oliver cemetery. Today, in Sarsfield Barracks, a monument erected by the soldiers of the Barracks stands at the place of his execution.

Appendix Five: The Senior Non-Commissioned Officers of the 12th Battalion

Sergeant Major 12th Infantry Battalion

BSM J. Noctor
BSM D. Lynch
BSM B. Dullard
BSM W. Kane
BSM A. Franklin
BSM C. Shanahan
BSM D. O'Keefe
BSM J. Dineen

Battalion Quartermaster Sergeant

BQMS J. Burke
BQMS J. Cullinane
BQMS N. Pearse
BQMS A. Kelleher
BQMS W. McNamara

APPENDIX SIX: DEFENCE FORCES ROLL OF HONOUR

IRISH DEFENCE FORCES PERSONNEL WHO DIED ON OVERSEAS MISSIONS

Congo

Coy Sgt	Grant, Felix (BSD)	3 October 1960
Col	McCarthy, Justin (BSD)	27 October 1960
Lt	Gleeson, Kevin	8 November 1960
Sgt	Gaynor, Hugh	8 November 1960
Cpl	Dougan, Liam	8 November 1960
Cpl	Kelly, Peter	8 November 1960
Pte	Farrell, Matthew	8 November 1960
Tpr	Fennell, Thomas	8 November 1960
Tpr	Browne, Anthony (BSD)	8 November 1960
Pte	McGuinn, Michael	8 November 1960
Pte	Killeen, Gerard	8 November 1960
Pte	Davis, Patrick	8 November 1960
Cpl	Kelly, Liam	24 December 1960
Cpl	Kelly, Luke	30 August 1961
Tpr	Gaffney, Edward	13 September 1961
Tpr	Mullins, Patrick	13 September 1961
Cpl	Nolan, Michael	15 September 1961
Cpl	Fallon, Michael	8 December 1961
Sgt	Mulcahy, Patrick (BSD)	16 December 1961
Lt	Riordan, Patrick (BSD)	16 December 1961
Pte	Wickham, Andrew	16 December 1961
Cpl	Geoghegan, John	28 December 1961
Cpl	Power, John	3 March 1962
Capt.	McCann, Ronald	9 May 1962
Cpl	McGrath, John	21 March 1963
Comdt	McMahon, Thomas	28 September 1963

Cyprus

Coy Sgt	McCauley, Wallace	22 February 1965
Sgt	Hamill, John	7 April 1965
Cpl	Heatherington, William	19 July 1965
Coy Sgt	Ryan, James	4 October 1966
Capt.	McNamara, Christopher	16 January 1968
Cpl	Fagan, James	10 June 1968
Lt	Byrne, Ronald	28 October 1968
Tpr	Kennedy, Michael	1 July 1969
Pte	Cummins, Brendan	11 June 1971

NTSO

| Comdt | Wickham, Thomas | 7 June 1967 |
| Comdt | Nestor, Michael | 25 September 1982 |

Lebanon

Pte	Moon, Gerard	25 August 1978
Cpl	Reynolds, Thomas	24 December 1978
Pte	Grogan, Philip	10 July 1979
Pte	Griffin, Stephen	14 April 1980
Pte	Smallhorn, Derek	18 April 1980
Pte	Barrett, Thomas	18 April 1980
Sgt	Yeates, Edward	31 May 1980
Cpl	Duffy, Vincent	18 October 1980
Pte	Marshall, John	17 December 1980
Coy Sgt	Martin, James	10 February 1981
Pte	Doherty, Hugh	27 April 1981
Pte	Seoighe, Caomhán	27 April 1981
Pte	Byrne, Niall	23 June 1981
Pte	Hodges, Gerard	20 March 1982
Pte	Burke, Peter	27 October 1982
Cpl	Morrow, Gregory	27 October 1982
Pte	Murphy, Thomas	27 October 1982
Cpl	Murray, George	9 October 1984
Tpr	Fogarty, Paul	20 July 1986
Lt	Murphy, Aonghus	21 August 1986
Pte	O'Brien, William	6 December 1986
Cpl	McLoughlin, Dermot	10 January 1987
RSM	Fitzgerald, John	24 February 1987
Cpl	Bolger, George	29 August 1987
Gnr	Cullen, Paul	17 March 1988
Pte	Wright, Patrick	21 August 1988
Pte	McNeela, Michael	24 February 1989
Cpl	Heneghan, Fintan	21 March 1989
Pte	Walsh, Thomas	21 March 1989
Pte	Armstrong, Mannix	21 March 1989

Sgt	Forrester, Charles	21 May 1989
Comdt	O'Hanlon, Michael	21 November 1989
Cpl	McCarthy, Michael	15 November 1991
Cpl	Ward, Peter	29 September 1992
Cpl	Tynan, Martin	13 December 1992
CQMS	Stokes, Kieran	14 June 1993
Airman	O'Connor, Stephen	3 October 1993
Sgt	Lynch, John	6 August 1997
Cpl	Dowling, Michael	16 September 1998
Pte	Barrett, Kevin	18 February 1999
Pte	Kedian, William	31 May 1999
Tpr	Campbell, Jonathan	5 September 1999
Pte	Deere, Declan	14 February 2000
Pte	Murphy, John	14 February 2000
Pte	Lawlor, Matthew	14 February 2000
Pte	Fitzpatrick, Brendan	14 February 2000

East Timor

| Pte | Ó Flathartha, Peadar | 15 April 2002 |

Liberia

| Sgt | Mooney, Derek | 27 November 2003 |

Appendix Seven: Deceased Personnel of Sarsfield Barracks

Listing of Regular personnel who died in service in Sarsfield Barracks as listed in the Garrison church

Sgt	D. O'Regan	February 1952	CQMS	J. Dillon	December 1976
Lt-Col.	J. Murphy	December 1952	Pte	R. Looney	March 1977
Cpl	P. Browne	December 1954	Pte	L. Fogarty	July 1977
Pte	P. O'Mahoney	July 1955	Col.	J.A. Reilly	August 1977
Pte	J. O'Brien	November 1956	Sgt	F. Moloney	July 1988
Sgt	P. Delaney	May 1959	Sgt	P. Daly	August 1979
Pte	P. Flynn	May 1960	Pte	J. Higgins	October 1979
Col.	J. Geoghegan	December 1961	Pte	G. Hanly	January 1980
Lt-Col.	J. Dundon	July 1962	Mr	S. McPhilips	November 1982
Sgt	J. Sheridan	January 1963	Pte	S. O'Connor	June 1986
Pte	M. Hickey	October 1963	Cpl	G. Bolger	August 1987
CQMS	R. Maguire	February 1964	Mr	W. Dillon	January 1988
Capt.	H. McCracken	March 1964	Cpl	E. Mason	October 1989
Pte	K. Hickey	November 1969	Pte	S. Rice	May 1990
Capt.	F. Warren	December 1969	Mr	J. McKnight	October 1990
CQMS	T. Murphy	June 1971	Sgt	F. O'Regan	August 1993
Coy Sgt	P. Neill	August 1972	Pte	P. Curtin	December 1995
Pte	J. McCormack	June 1972	Mr	Con Lenihan	December 1995
Comdt	M. Carroll	March 1973	Mr	F. Murphy	June 1997
Cpl	E. O'Toole	May 1973	CQMS	P. Ryan	April 1994
Pte	M. Whelan	March 1974	Sgt	J. O'Leary	September 1997
Comdt	P. O'Connell	July 1975	Pte	T. Boyce	June 2000
Cpl	P. Gardiner	January 1976	CQMS	B. Ryan	January 2001
Cpl	C. O'Brien	August 1976			

LISTING OF FCA PERSONNEL WHO DIED IN SERVICE IN SARSFIELD BARRACKS AS LISTED IN THE GARRISON CHURCH

Pte	A. Fitzgibbon	March 1967
Pte	J. McCarthy	January 1969
Pte	E. Moloney	July 1972
Pte	A. Barnes	July 1978
Pte	M. Lawlor	June 1979
Cpl	A. Shaw	June 1979
Pte	M. McInerney	November 1980
Pte	P. Hodnett	November 1982
Pte	R. Barry	December 1982
Pte	N. Sheehan	June 1984
Sgt	M. Brouder	June 1990
Coy Sgt	J. Kennedy	May 1992
Sgt	J. O'Reilly	October 1992
Sgt	C. McLoughlin	July 1995
Coy Sgt	R. Griffin	January 1998
Pte	C. Thompson	April 1999
Cpl	S. McGrath	August 2001
Pte	B. Gorey	April 2001
Comdt	P. Moroney	March 2002
Sgt	N. Shanahan	April 2004
Pte	G. Gordon	July 2004
Pte	A. Dawson	March 2005
Pte	D. Aherne	May 2005
Cpl	R. Slattery	July 2005

Appendix Eight: Unit Listing

This is a listing of units of the Irish Defence Forces, Free State Army and Anti-Treaty Republican Forces, and includes the names of unit commanders and officers who commanded the New Barracks/Sarsfield Barracks from 1922-2008, where possible. Attempts were also made to establish as far as possible the units of the Crown Forces who served in the New Barracks from 1798-1922. It is acknowledged that not all of the units may be included for this period. This list was compiled through research and references obtained from the following books: *In Search of the Forlorn Hope*, *History of the Irish Army* and *The Irish Sword*. Limerick trade directories were also examined. Army lists were located in National Archives Kew (UK), regimental websites, Irish Army Archives, local newspapers located in Mary Immaculate College (*Limerick Chronicle*, *Cork Examiner*) and records held in the Museum, Sarsfield Barracks.

2008

12th Inf Battalion, OC Lt-Col. L. Carroll.
31st Logistics Battalion Headquarters, RDF.
31st Logistics Battalion Medical Company, RDF.
31st Logistics Battalion Transport Company, RDF.
31st Logistics Battalion Engineer Coy, RDF.
32nd Inf Battalion. RDF.
31st Reserve Military Police Coy, RDF.
31st Reserve Communications Information, RDF.
3rd Air Defence Battery, RDF.
No. 5 Coy Naval Service Reserve.

2007

12th Inf Battalion, OC Lt-Col. M. Murray (Oct.) Lt-Col. L. Carroll.

31st Logistics Battalion Headquarters, RDF.
31st Logistics Battalion Medical Company, RDF.
31st Logistics Battalion Transport Company, RDF.
31st Logistics Battalion Engineer Coy, RDF.
32st Inf Battalion, RDF.
31st Reserve Military Police Coy, RDF.
31st Reserve Communications Information, RDF.
3rd Air Defence Battery, RDF.
No. 5 Coy Naval Service Reserve.

2006

12th Inf Battalion, OC Lt-Col. M. Murray.
31st Logistics Battalion Headquarters, RDF.
31st Logistics Battalion Medical Company, RDF.
31st Logistics Battalion Transport Company, RDF.
31st Logistics Battalion Engineer Coy, RDF.
32nd Inf Battalion, RDF.
31st Reserve Military Police Coy, RDF.
31st Reserve Communications Information, RDF.
No. 5 Coy Naval Service Reserve.
3rd Air Defence Battery, RDF.

2005

12th Inf Battalion, OC Lt-Col. M. McMahon (Sep.) Lt-Col. M. Murray. Southern Command FCA Headquarters, OC Lt-Col P. O'Brien (Oct., Headquarters moved to Kickham Barracks).
14th Inf Battalion FCA (Oct.).

3rd Field Military Police Company, FCA (Oct.).
3rd Field Engineer Company, FCA.
3rd Field Supply & Transport Company, FCA (Oct.).
3rd Field Medical Coy, FCA. (Oct.).
3rd Air Defence Battery, FCA. (Oct.).
3rd Field Signal Company, FCA. (Oct.).
No.5 Slua Muiri Coy (Oct.).
31st Logistics Battalion Headquarters, RDF.
31st Logistics Battalion Medical Company, RDF.
31st Logistics Battalion Transport Company, RDF.
31st Logistics Battalion Engineer Coy, RDF.
32nd Inf Battalion, RDF.
31st Reserve Military Police Coy, RDF.
31st Reserve Communications Information, RDF.
3rd Air Defence Battery, RDF.
No.5 Coy Naval Service Reserve.

2004

12th Inf Battalion, OC Lt-Col. M. McMahon.
Southern Command FCA Headquarters, OC Lt-Col. P. O'Brien.
14th Inf Battalion FCA.
3rd Field Military Police Company, FCA.
3rd Field Engineer Company, FCA.
3rd Field Supply & Transport Company, FCA.
3rd Field Medical Coy, FCA.
3 Air Defence Battery, FCA.
3rd Field Signal Company, FCA.
No.5 Slua Muiri Coy.

2003

12th Inf Battalion, OC Lt-Col. A.J. Daly (Mar.) Lt-Col. M. McMahon.
Southern Command FCA Headquarters, OC Lt-Col. P. O'Brien.
14th Inf Battalion FCA.
3rd Field Military Police Company, FCA.
3rd Field Engineer Company, FCA.
3rd Field Supply & Transport Company, FCA.
3rd Field Medical Coy, FCA.
3rd Air Defence Battery, FCA.
3rd Field Signal Company, FCA.
No.5 Slua Muiri Coy.

2002

12th Inf Battalion, OC Lt-Col. A.J. Daly.
Southern Command FCA Headquarters, OC Lt-Col. J.M. Scanlon (Jan.)
Lt-Co. P. O'Brien.
14th Inf Battalion FCA.
3rd Field Military Police Company, FCA.
3rd Field Engineer Company, FCA.
3rd Field Supply & Transport Company, FCA.
3rd Field Medical Coy, FCA.
3 Air Defence Battery, FCA.
3rd Field Signal Company, FCA.
No.5 Slua Muiri Coy.

2001

12th Inf Battalion, OC Lt-Col. M.P. O'Brien (Feb.) Lt-Col. A.J. Daly.
Southern Command FCA Headquarters, OC Lt-Col. J.M. Scanlon.
14th Inf Battalion FCA.
3rd Field Military Police Company, FCA.
3rd Field Engineer Company, FCA.
3rd Field Supply & Transport Company, FCA.
3rd Field Medical Coy, FCA.
3 Air Defence Battery, FCA.
3rd Field Signal Company, FCA.
No.5 Slua Muiri Coy.

2000

12th Inf Battalion, OC Lt-Col. MP. O'Brien.
Southern Command FCA Headquarters, OC Lt-Col. J.M. Scanlon.
14th Inf Battalion FCA.
3rd Field Military Police Company, FCA.
3rd Field Engineer Company, FCA.
3rd Field Supply & Transport Company, FCA.
3rd Field Medical Coy, FCA.
3 Air Defence Battery, FCA.
3rd Field Signal Company, FCA.
No.5 Slua Muiri Coy.

1999

12th Inf Battalion, OC Lt-Col. M.P. O'Brien.
Southern Command FCA Headquarters, OC Lt-Col. F.K. Jordan (Feb.) Lt-

Col. J.M. Scanlon.
14th Inf Battalion FCA.
3rd Field Military Police Company, FCA.
3rd Field Engineer Company, FCA.
3rd Field Supply & Transport Company, FCA.
3rd Field Medical Coy, FCA.
3 Air Defence Battery, FCA.
3rd Field Signal Company, FCA.
No.5 Slua Muiri Coy.

1998
12th Inf Battalion, OC Lt-Col. F. Swords (Aug.) Lt-Col. M.P. O'Brien.
Southern Command FCA Headquarters, OC Lt-Col. F.K. Jordan.
14th Inf Battalion FCA.
3rd Field Military Police Company, FCA.
3rd Field Engineer Company, FCA.
3rd Field Supply & Transport Company, FCA.
3rd Field Medical Coy, FCA.
3 Air Defence Battery, FCA.
3rd Field Signal Company, FCA.
No.5 Slua Muiri Coy.

1997
12th Inf Battalion, OC Lt-Col. C. Doyle (Sep.) Lt-Col. F. Swords.
Southern Command FCA Headquarters, OC Lt-Col. F.K. Jordan.
14th Inf Battalion FCA.
3rd Field Military Police Company, FCA.
3rd Field Engineer Company, FCA.
3rd Field Supply & Transport Company, FCA.
3rd Field Medical Coy, FCA.
3 Air Defence Battery, FCA.
3rd Field Signal Company, FCA.
No.5 Slua Muiri Coy.

1996
12th Inf Battalion, OC Lt-Col. C. Doyle.
Southern Command FCA Headquarters, OC Lt-Col. F.K. Jordan.
14th Inf Battalion FCA.
3rd Field Military Police Company, FCA.
3rd Field Engineer Company, FCA.

3rd Field Supply & Transport Company, FCA.
3rd Field Medical Coy, FCA.
3 Air Defence Battery, FCA.
3rd Field Signal Company, FCA.
No.5 Slua Muiri Coy.

1995
12th Inf Battalion, OC Lt-Col. J.F. Graham (Sept) Lt-Col. C. Doyle.
Southern Command FCA Headquarters, OC Lt-Col. J.E. Moriarty (Sep.) Lt-Col. F.K. Jordan.
14th Inf Battalion FCA.
3rd Field Military Police Company, FCA.
3rd Field Engineer Company, FCA.
3rd Field Supply & Transport Company, FCA.
3rd Field Medical Coy, FCA.
3 Air Defence Battery, FCA.
3rd Field Signal Company, FCA.
No.5 Slua Muiri Coy.

1994
12th Inf Battalion, OC Lt-Col. J.F. Graham.
Southern Command FCA Headquarters, OC Lt-Col. G. Staunton (Sep.) Lt-Col. J.E. Moriarty.
14th Inf Battalion FCA.
3rd Field Military Police Company, FCA.
3rd Field Engineer Company, FCA.
3rd Field Supply & Transport Company, FCA.
3rd Field Medical Coy, FCA.
3 Air Defence Bty, FCA.
3rd Field Signal Company, FCA.
No.5 Slua Muiri Coy.

1993
12th Inf Battalion OC Lt-Col. F.K. Jordan (Apr.) Lt- Col. J.F. Graham.
Southern Command FCA Headquarters, OC Lt-Col. P.J. McHale (Jan.) Lt-Col. G. Staunton.
14th Inf Battalion FCA.
3rd Field Military Police Company, FCA.
3rd Field Engineer Company, FCA.
3rd Field Supply & Transport Company, FCA.

3rd Field Medical Coy, FCA.
3 Air Defence Bty, FCA.
3rd Field Signal Company, FCA.
No. 5 Slua Muiri Coy.

1992
12th Inf Battalion, OC Lt-Col. W. Fitzgerald (Jan.) Lt-Col. F.K. Jordan.
Southern Command FCA Headquarters, OC Lt-Col. P.J. McHale.
14th Inf Battalion FCA.
3rd Field Military Police Company, FCA.
3rd Field Engineer Company, FCA.
3rd Field Supply & Transport Company, FCA.
3rd Field Medical Coy, FCA.
3 Air Defence Battery, FCA.
3rd Field Signal Company, FCA.
No. 5 Slua Muiri Coy.

1991
12th Inf Battalion, OC Lt-Col. W. Fitzgerald.
Southern Command FCA Headquarters, OC Col. B. O'Donovan (Feb.) Lt-Col. P.J. McHale.
14th Inf Battalion FCA.
3rd Field Military Police Company, FCA.
3rd Field Engineer Company, FCA.
3rd Field Supply & Transport Company, FCA.
3rd Field Medical Company, FCA.
3 Air Defence Battery, FCA.
3rd Field Signal Company, FCA.
No. 5 Slua Muiri Coy.

1990
12th Inf Battalion, OC Lt-Col. W. Fitzgerald.
Southern Command FCA Headquarters, OC Col. B. O'Donovan.
14th Inf Battalion FCA.
3rd Field Military Police Company, FCA.
3rd Field Engineer Company, FCA.
3rd Field Supply & Transport Company, FCA.
3rd Field Medical Company, FCA.
3 Air Defence Battery, FCA.
3rd Field Signal Company, FCA.

No. 5 Slua Muiri Coy.

1989
12th Inf Battalion, OC Lt-Col. J.J. Farrell (Jan.) Lt-Col. W. Fitzgerald.
Southern Command FCA Headquarters, OC Lt-Col. T. Dunne (Jan.) Col. B. O'Donovan.
14th Inf Battalion FCA.
3rd Field Military Police Company, FCA.
3rd Field Engineer Company, FCA.
3rd Field Supply & Transport Company, FCA.
3rd Field Medical Coy, FCA.
3 Air Defence Battery, FCA.
3rd Field Signal Company, FCA.
No. 5 Slua Muiri Company.

1988
12th Inf Battalion OC Lt-Col. O'Donovan (Mar.) Lt-Col. J.J. Farrell (May).
Southern Command FCA Headquarters, OC Col. L. O'Connor (Feb.) Col. A. McCarthy (Oct.) Lt-Col. T. Dunne.
14th Inf Battalion FCA.
3rd Field Military Police Company, FCA.
3rd Field Engineer Company, FCA.
3rd Field Supply & Transport Company, FCA.
3rd Field Medical Company, FCA.
3 Air Defence Battery, FCA.
3rd Field Signal Company, FCA.
No. 5 Slua Muiri Company.

1987
12th Inf Battalion, OC Lt-Col. J.J. Farrell (Oct.) Lt-Col. O'Donovan.
Southern Command FCA Headquarters, OC Col. L. O'Connor.
14th Inf Battalion FCA.
3rd Field Military Police Company, FCA.
3rd Field Engineer Company, FCA.
3rd Field Supply & Transport Company, FCA.
3rd Field Medical Company, FCA.
3 Air Defence Battery, FCA.
3rd Field Signal Company, FCA.
No. 5 Slua Muiri Company.

1986
12th Inf Battalion. OC Lt-Col. A. O'Riordan (Oct) Lt-Col. J.J. Farrell.
Southern Command FCA Headquarters, OC Col. L. O'Connor.
14th Inf Battalion FCA.
3rd Field Military Police Company, FCA.
3rd Field Engineer Company, FCA.
3rd Field Supply & Transport Company, FCA.
3rd Field Medical Company, FCA.
3rd Air Defence Battery, FCA.
3rd Field Signal Company, FCA.
No.5 Slua Muiri Company.

1985
12th Inf Battalion, OC Lt-Col. L.O'Connor.
Southern Command FCA Headquarters, OC Col. S. MacNoicaill (Apr.),
Col. T. Higgins (May) Col. L. O'Connor (Dec.).
14th Inf Battalion FCA.
3rd Field Military Police Company, FCA.
3rd Field Engineer Company, FCA.
3rd Field Supply & Transport Company, FCA.
3rd Field Medical Company, FCA.
3rd Air Defence Battery, FCA.
3rd Field Signal Company, FCA.
No.5 Slua Muiri Company.

1984
12th Inf Battalion, OC Lt-Col.. L. O'Connor.
Southern Command FCA Headquarters, OC Col. S. MacNoicaill.
14th Inf Battalion FCA.
3rd Field Military Police Company, FCA.
3rd Field Engineer Company, FCA.
3rd Field Supply & Transport Company, FCA.
3rd Field Medical Company, FCA.
3rd Air Defence Battery, FCA.
3rd Field Signal Company, FCA.
No.5 Slua Muiri Company.

1983
12th Inf Battalion, OC Lt-Col. P.J. Kelly (Nov.) Lt-Col. L. O'Connor.
Southern Command FCA Headquarters, OC Col. S. MacNoicaill.

14th Inf Battalion FCA.
3rd Field Military Police Company, FCA.
3rd Field Engineer Company, FCA.
3rd Field Supply & Transport Company, FCA.
3rd Field Medical Company, FCA.
3rd Air Defence Battery, FCA.
3rd Field Signal Company, FCA.
No.5 Slua Muiri Company.

1982
12th Inf Battalion, OC Lt-Col.. P.J. Kelly.
Southern Command FCA Headquarters, OC Col. J. Flynn (Mar.) Col. D.
O'Carroll (Apr.) Col. S. MacNoicaill (Jul).
14th Inf Battalion FCA.
3rd Field Military Police Company, FCA.
3rd Field Engineer Company, FCA.
3rd Field Supply & Transport Company, FCA.
3rd Field Medical Company, FCA.
3rd Air Defence Battery, FCA.
3rd Field Signal Company, FCA.
No.5 Slua Muiri Company, FCA.

1981
12th Inf Battalion, OC Lt-Col B. Cassidy (Mar) Lt-Col. S. MacNoicaill
(Apr) Lt-Col. P.J. Kelly.
Southern Command FCA Headquarters, OC Col. E. Russell (Jul) Col. T.
Carroll (Dec) Col. J. Flynn.
14th Inf Battalion FCA.
3rd Field Military Police Company, FCA.
3rd Field Engineer Company, FCA.
3rd Field Supply & Transport Company, FCA.
3rd Field Medical Company, FCA.
3rd Air Defence Battery, FCA.
3rd Field Signal Company, FCA.
No.5 Slua Muiri Company.

1980
12th Inf Battalion, OC Lt-Col. B. Cassidy.
Southern Command FCA Headquarters, OC Col. F. Dinneen (Oct.) Col.

E. Russell.
14th Inf Battalion FCA.
3rd Field Military Police Company, FCA.
3rd Field Engineer Company, FCA.
3rd Field Supply & Transport Company, FCA.
3rd Field Medical Coy, FCA.
3rd Air Defence Battery, FCA.
3rd Field Signal Company, FCA.
No. 5 Slua Muiri Coy.

1979
12th Inf Battalion, Lt-Col. T. Hartigan (Sep.), Lt-Col. B. Cassidy.
Southern Command FCA Headquarters, OC Col. F. Dinneen.
Headquarters 3rd Brigade, Southern Comd, OC Col. F. Dinneen.
14th Inf Battalion FCA.
3rd Field Military Police Company, FCA.
3rd Field Engineer Company, FCA.
3rd Field Supply & Transport Company, FCA.
3rd Field Medical Company, FCA.
3rd Air Defence Battery, FCA.
3rd Field Signal Company, FCA.
No. 5 Slua Muiri Company.

1978
12th Inf Battalion, Lt-Col. T. Hartigan.
Headquarters 3rd Brigade, Southern Comd, OC Col. F. Dinneen.
14th Inf Battalion FCA.
3rd Field Military Police Company, FCA.
3rd Field Engineer Company, FCA.
3rd Field Supply & Transport Company, FCA.
3rd Field Medical Company, FCA.
3rd Anti Aircraft Battery, FCA.
3rd Field Signal Company, FCA.
No. 5 Slua Muiri Company.

1977
12th Inf Battalion, OC Lt-Col. T. Hartigan.
Headquarters 3rd Brigade, Southern Comd, OC Col. M.K. Hanly (Aug.).
Col. F. Dinneen.
14th Inf Battalion FCA.

3rd Field Military Police Company, FCA.
3rd Field Engineer Company, FCA.
3rd Field Supply & Transport Company, FCA.
3rd Field Medical Company, FCA.
3rd Anti Aircraft Battery, FCA.
3rd Field Signal Company, FCA.
No. 5 Slua Muiri Company.

1976
12th Inf Battalion, OC Lt-Col. M. Power (Aug) Lt-Col. T. Hartigan.
Headquarters 3rd Brigade, Southern Comd, OC Col. M.K. Hanly.
14th Inf Battalion FCA.
3rd Field Military Police Company, FCA.
3rd Field Engineer Company, FCA.
3rd Field Supply & Transport Company, FCA.
3rd Field Medical Company, FCA.
3rd Anti Aircraft Battery, FCA.
3rd Field Signal Company, FCA.
No. 5 Slua Muiri Company.

1975
12th Inf Battalion, OC Lt-Col. M. Power.
Headquarters 3rd Brigade, Southern Comd, OC Col. P.P. Barry (Oct.) Col. M.K Hanly.
14th Inf Battalion, FCA.
3rd Field Military Police Company.
3rd Field Engineer Company.
3rd Field Supply & Transport Company.
3rd Field Medical Company.
3rd Anti Aircraft Battery, FCA.
3rd Field Signal Company.
No. 5 Slua Muiri Company.

1974
12th Inf Battalion, OC Lt-Col. M. Power.
Headquarters 3rd Brigade, Southern Comd, OC Col. P.P. Barry.
14th Inf Battalion FCA.
3rd Field Military Police Company, FCA.
3rd Field Engineer Company, FCA.
3rd Field Supply & Transport Company, FCA.

3rd Field Medical Company, FCA.
3rd Anti Aircraft Battery, FCA.
3rd Field Signal Company, FCA.
No.5 Slua Muiri Company.

1973
12th Inf Battalion, OC Lt-Col. M. Power.
Headquarters 3rd Brigade, Southern Comd, OC Col. P.P. Barry.
14th Inf Battalion, FCA.
3rd Field Military Police Company, FCA.
3rd Field Engineer Company, FCA.
3rd Field Supply & Transport Company, FCA.
3rd Field Medical Company, FCA.
3rd Anti Aircraft Battery, FCA.
3rd Field Signal Company, FCA.
No.5 Slua Muiri Company.

1972
12th Inf Battalion, OC Lt-Col. B.G. McGuirk (Jan.) Lt-Col. M. Power.
Headquarters 3rd Brigade Southern Comd (Jul.) OC Col. P.P. Barry.
14th Inf Battalion, FCA.
3rd Field Military Police Company, FCA.
3rd Field Engineer Company, FCA.
3rd Field Supply & Transport Company, FCA.
3rd Field Medical Company, FCA.
3rd Anti Aircraft Battery, FCA.
3rd Field Signal Company, FCA.
No.5 Slua Muiri Company.

1971
12th Inf Battalion, OC Lt-Col. B.G. McGuirk.
Headquarters 3rd Brigade Southern Comd.
14th Inf Battalion FCA.
3rd Field Military Police Company, FCA.
3rd Field Engineer Company, FCA.
3rd Field Supply & Transport Company, FCA.
3rd Field Medical Company, FCA.
3rd Anti Aircraft Battery, FCA.
3rd Field Signal Company, FCA.
No.5 Slua Muiri Company.

1969
12th Inf Battalion, OC Lt-Col.l B.G. McGuirk.
Headquarters 3rd Brigade Southern Comd.
14th Inf Battalion FCA.
3rd Field Military Police Company.
3rd Field Engineer Company.
3rd Field Supply & Transport Company.
3rd Field Medical Coy.
3rd Anti Aircraft Battery, FCA.
3rd Field Signal Company.
No.5 Slua Muiri Coy.

1968
12th Inf Battalion, OC Lt-Col. B.G. McGuirk.
Headquarters 3rd Brigade, Southern Comd, OC Col. J. Fitzsimons (Jun.).
14th Inf Battalion FCA.
3rd Field Military Police Company.
3rd Field Engineer Company.
3rd Field Supply & Transport Company.
3rd Field Medical Coy.
3rd Anti Aircraft Battery, FCA.
3rd Field Signal Company.

1967
12th Inf Battalion, OC Lt-Col. B.G. McGuirk.
Headquarters 3rd Brigade Southern Comd.
14th Inf Battalion FCA.
3rd Field Military Police Company.
3rd Field Engineer Company.
3rd Field Supply & Transport Company.
3rd Field Medical Coy.
3rd Anti Aircraft Battery, FCA.
3rd Field Signal Company.
No.5 Slua Muiri Coy.

1966
12th Inf Battalion, OC Lt-Col. J.K. Mc Mahon (May) Lt-Col. B.G. McGuirk.
Headquarters 3rd Brigade, Southern Comd, OC Col. J. Fitzsimons.
14th Inf Battalion FCA.
3rd Field Military Police Company, FCA.
3rd Field Engineer Company, FCA.
3rd Field Supply & Transport Company, FCA.
3rd Field Medical Coy, FCA.
3rd Anti Aircraft Battery, FCA.
3rd Field Signal Company, FCA.
No.5 Slua Muiri Coy.

1965
12th Inf Battalion, OC Lt-Col. B.G. McGuirk (Oct.) Lt-Col. J.K. Mc Mahon.
Headquarters 3rd Brigade Southern Comd.
14th Inf Battalion, FCA.
3rd Field Military Police Company, FCA.
3rd Field Engineer Company, FCA.
3rd Field Supply & Transport Company, FCA.
3rd Field Medical Company, FCA.
3rd Anti Aircraft Battery, FCA.
3rd Field Signal Company, FCA.
No.5 Slua Muiri Coy.

1964
12th Inf Battalion, OC Lt-Col. P.P. Barry (Jun.) Lt-Col. B.G. McGuirk.
Headquarters 3rd Brigade, Southern Comd, OC Col. J. Fitzsimons.
14th Inf Battalion FCA.
3rd Field Military Police Company, FCA.
3rd Field Engineer Company, FCA.
3rd Field Supply & Transport Company, FCA.
3rd Field Medical Company, FCA.
3rd Anti Aircraft Battery, FCA.
3rd Field Signal Company, FCA.
No.5 Slua Muiri Coy.

1963
12th Inf Battalion, OC Lt-Col. P.P. Barry.

Headquarters 3rd Brigade, Southern Comd, OC Col. J. Fitzsimons.
14th Inf Battalion FCA.
3rd Field Military Police Company, FCA.
3rd Field Engineer Company, FCA.
3rd Field Supply & Transport Company, FCA.
3rd Field Medical Company, FCA.
3rd Anti Aircraft Battery, FCA.
3rd Field Signal Company, FCA.
No.5 Slua Muiri Coy.

1962
12th Inf Battalion, OC Lt-Col. J. Reilly (Jul.) Lt-Col. P.P. Barry.
Headquarters 3rd Brigade, Southern Comd, OC Col. J. Fitzsimons.
14th Inf Battalion, FCA.
3rd Field Military Police Company, FCA.
3rd Field Engineer Company, FCA.
3rd Field Supply & Transport Company, FCA.
3rd Anti Aircraft Battery, FCA.
3rd Field Signal Company, FCA.
No.5 Slua Muiri Coy.

1961
12th Inf Battalion, OC Lt-Col. J. Reilly.
Headquarters 3rd Brigade, Southern Comd OC Col. J. Fitzsimons.
3rd Field Engineers Company, FCA.
3rd Field Signals Company, FCA.
3rd Field Supply & Transport Company, FCA.
3rd Anti Aircraft Battery, FCA.
No.5 Slua Muiri Coy.

1960
12th Inf Battalion, OC Lt-Col. J. Reilly.
Headquarters 3rd Brigade Southern Comd, OC Col. D. Kelly (Jul) Col. J. Fitzsimons.
3rd Field Engineers Company, FCA.
3rd Field Signals Company, FCA.
3rd Field Supply & Transport Company, FCA.
3rd Anti Aircraft Battery, FCA.
No.5 Slua Muiri Coy.

1959
12th Inf Battalion, OC Lt-Col. J. Dundon (Oct.), Lt-Col. J. Reilly
49th Inf Battalion, FCA.
Headquarters 3rd Brigade Southern Comd. OC Col. D. Kelly (Oct.).
3rd Field Engineers Company, FCA.
3rd Field Signals Company, FCA.
3rd Field Supply & Transport Company, FCA.
3rd Anti Aircraft Battery, FCA.
No.5 Slua Muiri Coy.

1958
12th Inf Battalion, OC Lt-Col. J. Dundon.
49th Inf Battalion FCA.
No.5 Slua Muiri Coy.

1955
12th Inf Battalion, OC Lt-Col. J. Healy.
49th Inf Battalion FCA.
No.5 Slua Muiri Coy.

1954
12th Inf Battalion, OC Lt-Col. J. Healy.
49th Inf Battalion FCA.
No.5 Slua Muiri Coy.

1953
12th Inf Battalion, OC Lt-Col. J. Healy.
49th Inf Battalion FCA.
No.5 Slua Muiri Coy.

1952
12th Inf Battalion, OC Lt-Col. J. Healy.
49th Inf Battalion FCA.
No.5 Slua Muiri Coy.

1951
12th Inf Battalion , OC Lt-Col. J.P. Murphy.
49th Inf Battalion FCA.
No.5 Slua Muiri Coy.

1950
12th Inf Battalion , OC Lt-Col. J.P. Murphy.
49th Inf Battalion FCA.
No.5 Slua Muiri Coy.

1949
12th Inf Battalion , OC Lt-Col. J.P. Murphy.
49th Inf Battalion FCA.
No.5 Slua Muiri Coy.

1948
12th Inf Battalion, OC Lt-Col. J.P. Murphy.
49th Inf Battalion FCA.
No.5 Slua Muiri Coy.

1947
12th Inf Battalion, OC Lt-Col. M.L. Higgins (Feb.), Lt-Col. J.P. Murphy.
49th Inf Battalion FCA.
No.5 Slua Muiri Coy.

1946
12th Inf Battalion, OC Lt-Col. S. McKeown (Mar.), Lt-Col. M.L. Higgins.
49th Inf Battalion FCA.

1945
Head quarters 7th Brigade, OC Col. Tom Feeney.
7th Field Artillery Regiment (3,17,18 Batteries).
7th Field Signals Coy.
7th Engineers Coy.
7th Field Supply & Transport Coy.

1944
Head quarters 7th Brigade, OC Col. T. Feeney.
7th Field Artillery Regiment (3,17,18 Batteries).
7th Field Signals Coy.
7th Engineers Coy.
7th Field Supply & Transport Coy.

1943
Head quarters 7th Brigade, OC Col. T. Feeney.

7th Field Artillery Regiment (3,17,18 Batteries).
7th Field Signals Coy.
7th Engineers Coy.
7th Field Supply & Transport Coy.

1942
Head quarters 7th Brigade, OC Col. T. Feeney.
7th Field Artillery Regiment (3,17,18 Batteries).
7th Field Signals Coy.
7th Engineers Coy.
7th Field Supply & Transport Coy.

1941
Head quarters 7th Brigade, OC Col. T. Feeney.
7th Field Artillery Regiment (3,17,18 Batteries).
7th Field Signals Coy.
7th Engineers Coy.
7th Field Supply & Transport Coy.

1940
Head quarters 7th Brigade.
7th Field Artillery Regiment (3,17,18 Batteries).
7th Field Signals Coy.
7th Engineers Coy.
7th Field Supply & Transport Coy.

1939
9th Inf Battalion, OC Lt-Col. T. Halpin.
Thomond Regiment.
New designated Barracks staff, Limerick.

1938
Volunteer Reserve training centre.
Thomond Regiment.
New designated Barracks staff, Limerick.

1937
Volunteer Reserve training centre.
Thomond Regiment.
New designated Barracks staff, Limerick.

1936
Volunteer Reserve training centre.
Thomond Regiment.
New designated Barracks staff, Limerick.

1935
Volunteer Reserve training centre, OC Comdt T. Crean.
Thomond Regiment.
New designated Barracks staff, Limerick.

1934
Thomond Regiment.
New designated Barracks staff, Limerick.

1930
4th Battalion.

1929
4th Inf Battalion OC Major T. Ryan.

1928
Limerick Military District.
4th Brigade HQ OC Col Edward Vile.

1927
Limerick Military District.
4th Brigade HQ OC Col Edward Vile.

1926
14th Battalion OC Comdt Isaih Convoy.

1925
14th Battalion OC Comdt Isaih Convoy.

1924
Headquarters 4th Brigade.
14th Battalion OC Comdt Isaih Convoy.

1923
Limerick Command Head Quarters, Gen. Michael Brennan.

7th Inf Battalion OC Comdt L. Walsh.

1922
IRA Field General Headquarters, OC Gen. Liam Lynch.
1st Western Division Free State Army, OC Gen. Michael Brennan.
4th Southern Division Free State Army, OC Gen. O'Hannigan.
23rd Regiment of Foot, 2nd Battalion The Royal Welch Fusiliers.
12th Field Company Royal Engineers.
B' Mobile Searchlight Group Royal Engineers.
Headquarters 18th Infantry Brigade.

1921
Headquarters 18th Infantry Brigade.
23rd Regiment of Foot, 2nd Battalion The Royal Welch Fusiliers.

1920
1st Battalion, The Royal Green Jackets.
Headquarters 18th Infantry Brigade.
23rd Regiment of Foot, 2nd Battalion The Royal Welch Fusiliers.

1919
23rd Regiment of Foot, 2nd Battalion The Royal Welch Fusiliers.
Headquarters 18th Infantry Brigade.

1918
3rd Battalion Royal Welch Fusiliers.
The Royal Sussex Regiment, 1/6th cyclist Battalion (Territorial force).

1917
3rd Battalion Royal Welch Fusiliers.

1916
4th Battalion Leinster Regiment.

1915
Royal Army Medical Corp, 32nd Field Ambulance Regiment.

1914
2nd Battalion, The York and Lancaster Regiment.

1913
The York and Lancaster Regiment, OC Lt-Col. Cobbold Ernest Cazenove.

1912
2nd Battalion, Royal Munster Fusiliers.

1911
2nd Battalion, Royal Munster Fusiliers.

1910
2nd Battalion, Royal Munster Fusiliers.

1909
2nd Battalion, Royal Munster Fusiliers, OC Major R.C. Boyle.
1st Battalion Black Watch.

1908
2nd Battalion, Royal Munster Fusiliers, OC Lt-Col. Bryce Stewart.
1st Battalion The Black Watch (Royal Highland Regiment).

1907
2nd Battalion, Royal Munster Fusiliers, OC Lt-Col. Bryce Stewart.

1906
4th Battalion, Northumberland Fusiliers, OC Lt-Col. William Sitwell.

1905
4th Battalion, Northumberland Fusiliers, OC Lt-Col. William Sitwell.

1904
2nd Battalion, King's (Liverpool) Regiment, OC Lt-Col. O'Donnel Gratten.

1903
2nd Battalion, King's (Liverpool) Regiment, OC Lt-Col. O'Donnel Gratten.

1902
1st Battalion, King's Own Yorkshire Light Infantry, OC Sir Henry Allen Johnson.
2nd Battalion, King's (Liverpool) Regiment, OC Lt-Col. O'Donnel Gratten.

1901
1st Battalion, King's Own Yorkshire Light Infantry, OC Lt-Col. Charles St Leger Barter.

1900
1st Battalion, King's Own Yorkshire Light Infantry, OC Lt-Col. Charles St Leger Barter.
17th Cancers.

1899
2nd Battalion, The Cheshire Regiment, OC Lt-Col. William Frederick Curteis.
17th Cancers.

1898
2nd Battalion, The Cheshire Regiment, OC Lt-Col. William Frederick Curteis.
1st Battalion, The Royal Irish Regiment, OC Lt-Col. John Henry Spyer.
17th Cancers.

1897
1st Battalion, The Royal Irish Regiment, OC Lt-Col. John Henry Spyer.
8th Royal Irish Hussars.

1896
1st Battalion, The Royal Irish Regiment, OC Lt-Col. John Henry Spyer.
14th Hussars.

1895
1st Battalion, The Royal Irish Regiment, OC Lt-Col. John Henry Spyer.
1st Battalion, the Manchester Regiment, OC Lt-Col. HC Marryat.

1894
1st Battalion, The Royal Irish Regiment, OC Lt-Col. John Henry Spyer.
1st Battalion, The Manchester Regiment, OC Lt-Col. H.C. Marryat.
14th Hussars and 15th Hussars.

1893
1st Battalion, The Manchester Regiment, OC Lt-Col. H.C. Marryat.
10th Hussars.

1892
2nd Battalion, The Black Watch (Royal Highland Regiment) OC Lt-Col H. Gunter.

1891
2nd Battalion, The Black Watch (Royal Highland Regiment) OC Lt-Col H. Gunter.
15th Kings Hussars.
2nd Battalion, Worcestershire Regiment, OC Lt-Col. H.J. de Berniere.

1890
2nd Battalion, Worcestershire Regiment, OC Lt-Col. H.J. de Berniere.

1889
2nd Battalion Worchestershire Regiment, OC Lt-Col. H.J. de Berniere.
2nd Battalion The Chesire Regiment.
1st Battalion The Sherwood Foresters.
3rd Hussars.

1888
2nd Battalion Leinster Regiment.
1st Battalion The Sherwood Foresters.
3rd Hussars.

1887
2nd Battalion Leinster Regiment.
3rd Hussars.

1886
2nd Battalion Leinster Regiment.
18th Hussars.
21st Hussars.

1885
The Kings Royal Rifle Corp.
Leicestershire & Rutland Regiment of Foot.
21st Hussars

1884
2nd Battalion, The Royal Green Jackets.

1st Battalion, The King's Rifle Corps.

1883
2nd Battalion Oxfordshire and Buckinghamshire Light Infantry.
2nd Dragoon Guards (Queens Bay).

1882
1st Battalion, The Duke of Cambridge's Own (Middlesex) Regt.
OC Lt-Col. James Richard Know Tredennick.
9th Royal Norfolk Regiment.
2nd Dragoon Guards.

1881
57th Regiment of Foot (West Middlesex), OC Lt-Col. James Richard Know Tredennick.

1880
19th Hussars.
87th Regiment of Foot (Royal Irish Fusiliers), OC Lt-Col. Nathanial Stevenson.
Depôt Battalion (64th & 98th Regiments of Foot linked Battalion).
9th Regiment (Norfolk).

1879
82nd Regiment of Foot (The Prince of Wales Volunteers), OC Lt-Col. Francis Dalrymple Walters.
87th Regiment of Foot (Royal Irish Fusiliers).
Depôt Battalion (64th & 98th Regiments of Foot linked Battalion).
3rd King's Own Hussars.

1878
82nd Regiment of Foot (The Prince of Wales Volunteers), OC Lt-Col. William Grogan Graves.
Depôt Battalion (64th & 98th Regiments of Foot linked Battalion).

1877
90th Regiment of Foot (Perthshire Volunteers) (Light Infantry), OC Lt-Col. Henry Wellington Palmer.
82nd Regiment of Foot (The Prince of Wales, Volunteers).
5th (Princess Charlotte of Wales) Dragoon Guards.

87th Regiment of Foot (Royal Irish Fusiliers).
Depôt Battalion (64th & 98th Regiments of Foot linked Battalion).
2nd Dragoon Guards.

1876
46th Regiment of Foot (South Devonshire), OC Lt-Col. Charles Parker Catty.
5th (Princess Charlotte of Wales) Dragoon Guards.
3rd Regiment of Foot (The East Kent).
87th Regiment of Foot (Royal Irish Fusiliers).
Depôt Battalion (64th & 98th Regiments of Foot linked Battalion).
90th Regiment of Foot (Perthshire Volunteers).

1875
3rd Regiment of Foot (The East Kent) OC Lt-Col. Talbot Ashley Cox.
87th Regiment of Foot (Royal Irish Fusiliers).
Depôt Battalion (64th & 98th Regiments of Foot linked Battalion).
46th Regiment of Foot (South Devonshires).

1874
64th Regiment of Foot (2nd Staffordshire), OC Lt-Col. Thomas de Courcy Hamilton.
3rd The Buffs Royal East Kent.
Depôt Battalion (joint 64th & 98th Regiments of Foot).
98th Regiment of Foot (Prince of Wales).

1873
64th Regiment of Foot (2nd Staffordshire), OC Lt-Col. Thomas de Courcy Hamilton.
3rd Regiment of Foot (The East Kent).
87th Regiment of Foot (Royal Irish Fusiliers).
Depôt Battalion (94th Regiment of Foot).
98th Regiment of Foot (Regiment of Wales).

1872
57th Regiment of Foot (The West Middlesex), OC Lt-Col. Edward Bowen.
87th Regiment of Foot (Royal Irish Fusiliers).

1871
57th Regiment of Foot (The West Middlesex), OC Lt-Col. Edward Bowen.
87th Regiment of Foot (Royal Irish Fusiliers).

1870
70th Regiment of Foot (Surrey), OC Lt-Col. William Cooper.
89th Regiment of Foot (The Princess Victoria's).

1869
72nd Regiment of Foot (Duke of Albany's Own Highlanders), OC Lt-Col. William Payn.

1868
6th Dragoons.
52nd Regiment of Foot (Oxfordshire), OC Lt-Col. Arthur Lennox Peel.
72nd Regiment of Foot (Duke of Albany's Own Highlanders).

1867
6th Dragoons.
74th Regiment of Foot (Highland), OC Lt-Col. William Kelty MacLeod.
52nd Regiment of Foot (Oxfordshire), OC Lt-Col. Arthur Lennox Peel.

1866
73rd Regiment of Foot (Perthshire), OC Lt-Col. Godfrey James Burne.
74th Regiment of Foot (Highland), OC Lt-Col. William Kelty MacLeod.
12th Cancer.
6th Dragoon Guards.

1865
12th Depôt Battalion, OC Lt-Col. Arthur Cyril Goodenough.
Depôt of 106th Regiment of Foot (Bombay European Light Infantry).
106th Regiment of Foot (Bombay European Light Infantry).

1864
17th Depôt Battalion, OC Lt-Col. Arthur Bordon.
74th Regiment of Foot (Highland).

1863
17th Depôt Battalion, OC Lt-Col. Arthur Bordon.
9th Regiment of Foot (Norfolk).

1862
17th Depôt Battalion, OC Lt-Col. Arthur Bordon.

1861
17th Depôt Battalion, OC Lt-Col. Arthur Bordon.
Depôt, 3rd Regiment of Foot (The East Kent).

1860
17th Depôt Battalion, OC Lt-Col. Arthur Bordon.

1859
Limerick Depôt Battalion, OC Lt-Col. Arthur Bordon.
13th Regiment of Foot (The 1st Somersetshire) (Prince Albert's Light Infantry).
68th Regiment of Foot (Durham).

1858
Limerick Depôt Battalion, OC Lt-Col. Nathanial Massey Stack.
Depôt, 3rd Regiment of Foot (The East Kent).
Depôt, 9th Regiment of Foot (The East Norfolk).
Depôt, 17th Regiment of Foot (The Leicestershire).

1857
Provisional Depôt Battalion, OC Lt-Col. Nathanial Massey Stack.
Depôt, 9th Regiment of Foot (The East Norfolk).
Depôt, 16th Regiment of Foot (The Bedfordshire).
Depôt, 17th Regiment of Foot (The Leicestershire).
Depôt, 39th Regiment of Foot (The Dorsetshire).
3rd Regiment of Foot (The East Kent).

1856
Provisional Depôt Battalion, OC Lt-Col. Nathanial Massey Stack.
Depôt, 9th Regiment of Foot (The East Norfolk).
Depôt, 17th Regiment of Foot (The Leicestershire).
Depôt, 39th Regiment of Foot (The Dorsetshire).
Depôt, 89th Regiment of Foot (The Princess Victoria's).

1855
Provisional Depôt Battalion, OC Lt-Col. Nathanial Massey Stack.
Depôt, 9th Regiment of Foot (The East Norfolk).
Depôt, 17th Regiment of Foot (The Leicestershire).
Depôt, 72nd Regiment of Foot (Duke of Albany's Own Highlanders).

1854

Headquarters, 14th Regiment of Foot (The Buckinghamshire), OC Lt-Col. Maurice Barlow.

West Yorkshire Prince of Wales's Own.

72nd Regiment of Foot (Duke of Albany's Own Highlanders).

1853

Headquarters, 14th Regiment of Foot (The Buckinghamshire), OC Lt-Col. Maurice Barlow.

Depôt, 47th Regiment of Foot (The Lancashire).

West Yorkshire Prince of Wales's Own.

1852

Headquarters, 52nd Regiment of Foot (Oxfordshire), OC Lt-Col. Cecil William Forester.

Headquarters, 63rd Regiment of Foot (The West Suffolk), OC Lt-Col. Arthur Cunliffe.

1851

Headquarters, 68th Regiment of Foot (Durham), OC Lt-Col. Richard William Huey.

Headquarters, 52nd Regiment of Foot (Oxfordshire).

The Royal Scots (Lothian Regiment).

63rd Regiment of Foot (The West Suffolk).

Depôt, 3rd Regiment of Foot (The East Kent).

1850

Headquarters, 3rd Regiment of Foot (The East Kent) OC Lt-Col. Sir James Dennis.

Headquarters, 74th Regiment of Foot (Highland), OC Lt-Col. John Fordyce.

68th Regiment of Foot (Durham).

1849

Headquarters, 3rd Regiment of Foot (The East Kent), OC Lt-Col. Sir James Dennis.

Headquarters, 47th Regiment of Foot (Lancashire) OC Lt-Col. Philip Dundas.

Headquarters, 92nd Regiment of Foot (Highland) OC Lt-Col. John Forbes.

1848

3rd Regiment of Foot (The East Kent).

64th Regiment of Foot (2nd Staffordshire).

92nd Regiment of Foot (Gordon Highlanders).

1847

55th Regiment of Foot (Westmoreland).

59th Regiment of Foot (2nd Nottinghamshire).

74th Regiment of Foot (Highland).

1846

24th Regiment of Foot (2nd Warwickshire).

83rd Regiment of Foot (County of Dublin).

85th Regiment of Foot (The Kings Light Infantry).

1845

24th Regiment of Foot (2nd Warwickshire).

15th Regiment of Foot (The Yorkshire East Riding).

1844

61st Regiment of Foot (South Gloucestershire).

30th Regiment of Foot (Cambridgeshire).

1843

36th Regiment of Foot (Herefordshire).

1842

84th Regiment of Foot (York & Lancaster).

5th Princess Charlotte of Wales Dragoons.

1841

37th Regiment of Foot (The North Hampshire).

20th Regiment of Foot (The East Devonshire), OC Col. Thomas.

84th Regiment of Foot (York and Lancaster).

5th Princess Charlotte of Wales Dragoons.

Depôt, 97th Regiment of Foot (The Earl of Ulster).

1840

42nd Regiment of Foot (Royal Highland).

1839
92nd Regiment of Foot (Gordon Highlanders).
Depôt, 70th Regiment of Foot (Surrey).
10th Regiment of Foot (The North Lincolnshire).
42nd Regiment of Foot (Royal Highland).

1838
25th Regiment of Foot (The York).

1837
21st Regiment of Foot (Royal Scots Fusiliers).

1836
94th Regiment of Foot.

1835
7th Dragoon Guards.
18th Regiment of Foot (Royal Irish).
15th (The Kings) Hussars.
30th Regiment of Foot (Cambridgeshire).

1834
18th Regiment of Foot (The Royal Irish).
91st Regiment of Foot (Princess Louise's Argyllshire).

1833
83 rd Regiment of Foot (County of Dublin).
85th Regiment of Foot (The Kings Light Infantry).

1832
9th Regiment of Foot (East Norfolk).
27th Regiment of Foot (Inniskilling).
83rd Regiment of Foot (County of Dublin).

1831
71st Regiment of Foot (Highland).
56th Regiment of Foot (The West Essex).
74th Regiment of Foot (Highland).

1830
56th Regiment of Foot (The West Essex).
60th Regiment of Foot King's Royal Rifle Corps.
62nd Regiment of Foot (The Wiltshire).

1829
60th Regiment of Foot, King's Royal Rifle Corps.
36th Regiment of Foot (Herefordshire).

1828
32nd Regiment of Foot (Cornwall).
37th Regiment of Foot (North Hampshire).

1827
66th Regiment of Foot. (Berkshire).

1826
24th Regiment of Foot (2nd Warwickshire).
37th Regiment of Foot (North Hampshire).
22nd Regiment of Foot (The Chesire).

1825
22nd Regiment of Foot (The Cheshire).
61st Regiment of Foot (South Gloucestershire).
88th Regiment of Foot (Connaught Rangers).
19th Regiment of Foot (1st Yorkshire North Riding – Princess of Wales Own).

1824
39th Regiment of Foot (Dorsetshire).
Rifle Brigade (Prince Consorts's Own).

1823
42nd Regiment of Foot (Royal Highland).
43rd Regiment of Foot (Monmouthshire).
39th Regiment of Foot (Dorsetshire).
93rd Regiment of Foot (Sutherland Highlanders).
2nd Battalion Rifle Brigade.
94th Regiment of Foot.

1822
40th Regiment of Foot (2nd Somersetshire).
57th Regiment of Foot (The West Middlesex).
42nd Regiment of Foot (Royal Highland).
6th Dragoons.
3rd King's Own Hussars.

1821
57th Regiment of Foot (The West Middlesex).
93rd Regiment of Foot (Sutherland Highlanders), OC Col. Gorden.
79th Regiment of Foot (The Queens Own Cameron Highlanders).
3rd King's Own Hussars.

1820
12th Regiment of Foot (The East Suffolk).
23rd Regiment of Foot (Royal Welch Fusiliers).
79th Regiment of Foot (The Queen's Own Cameron Highlanders).

1819
11th Regiment of Foot (The North Devonshire).

1818
74th Regiment of Foot (Highland).
77th Regiment of Foot (The East Middlesex).
87th Regiment of Foot (Royal Irish Fusiliers).
93rd Regiment of Foot (Sutherland Highlanders).

1817
74th Regiment of Foot (Highland).
77th Regiment of Foot (The East Middlesex).
93rd Regiment of Foot (Sutherland Highlanders).
6th Dragoon Guards (Carabiniers).

1816
30th Regiment of Foot (Cambridgeshire).
74th Regiment of Foot (Highland).
77th Regiment of Foot (East Middlesex).
84th Regiment of Foot (York & Lancaster).
93rd Regiment of Foot (Sutherland Highlanders).

1815
48th Regiment of Foot (The Northamptonshire).
30th Regiment of Foot (Cambridgeshire).
91st Regiment of Foot (Princess Louise's Argyllshire).
71st Regiment of Foot (Highland).
74th Regiment of Foot (Highland).
93rd Regiment of Foot (Sutherland Highlanders).

1814
91st Regiment of Foot (Princess Louise's Argyllshire).

1813
23rd Regiment of Foot (Royal Welch Fusiliers).
9th Regiment of Foot (East Norfolk).

1812
90th Regiment of Foot (Perthshire Volunteers).

1811
90th Regiment of Foot (Perthshire Volunteers).

1810
1st King's (German) Dragoons.
The North Cork Militia.
The Waterford Militia.

1809
7th (Princess Royal) Dragoon Guards.
The North Cork Militia.
The Waterford Militia.

1808
31st Regiment of Foot (Huntingdonshire).
53rd Regiment of Foot (Shropshire).
7th (Princess Royal) Dragoon Guards.

1807
53rd Regiment of Foot (Shropshire).
69th Regiment of Foot (South Lincolnshire).

1806
53rd Regiment of Foot (Shropshire).
69th Regiment of Foot (South Lincolnshire).
18th Royal Hussars (Queen Mary's Own).

1805
48th Regiment of Foot (Northamptonshire).
53rd Regiment of Foot (Shropshire).
18th Royal Hussars (Queen Mary's Own).

1804
45th Regiment of Foot (Nottinghamshire).
71st Regiment of Foot (Highland).

1803
56th Regiment of Foot (West Essex).
17th Regiment of Foot (Leicestershire).
71st Regiment of Foot (Highland).

1802
46th Regiment of Foot (South Devonshire).

1806
16th Regiment of Foot (Bedfordshire).

1801
46th Regiment of Foot (South Devonshire).

1800
46th Regiment of Foot (South Devonshire).
54th Regiment of Foot (West Norfolk).
56th Regiment of Foot (West Essex).

1799
9th Regiment of Foot (Norfolk).
68th Regiment of Foot (Durham Light Infantry).
41st Regiment of Foot (Welch).

1798
68th Regiment of Foot (Durham Light Infantry).
89th Regiment of Foot (The Princess Victoria's).

1797
9th Regiment of Foot (Norfolk Regiment).

Appendix Nine: Additional Regiments raised in Limerick during this period

135th Regiment of Foot (Limerick) was an Infantry Regiment of the British Army created and promptly disbanded in 1796. Raised by Sir Vere Hunt, the regiment saw no active service. It served solely to recruit soldiers. On disbandment, the recruits were drafted into other regiments. The regiment has the interesting historical distinction of having had the highest regimental number of any British line regiment.

134th Regiment of Foot (Loyal Limerick) was an Infantry Regiment of the British Army created in 1794 and disbanded in 1796. The regiment was formed in Ireland by re-designating the newly raised 2nd Battalion of the 83rd Regiment of Foot and did not leave Ireland before being disbanded in 1796. The Limerick City Regiment was established in 1793. In 1798, they fought Hiberno-French forces at Collooney, Co. Sligo (1798 Rebellion).

5th Battalion Royal Munster Fusiliers formed from the remains of the Limerick City Militia as a reserve battalion of the Munster Fusiliers in 1881. They were called to full-time service in August 1914. The battalion was located at Strand Barracks, moved to Scotland in November 1917 and was absorbed by the 3rd Battalion in May 1918.

FURTHER READING

Bartlett, T. & Jeffery, K., *A Military History of Ireland* (Cambridge, 1997).

Douet, James, *British Barracks, 1600-1914: Their Architecture and Role in Society* (London, 1998).

Kerrigan, P., *Castles and Fortifications in Ireland, 1485-1945* (Cork, 1995).

Lenihan, M. Esq., *Limerick: Its History and Antiquities, Ecclesiastical, Civil, and Military*, ed. Cian O'Carroll (Cork, 1991).

About the Authors

Corporal William Sheehan currently serves with the 31st Reserve Military Police Company in Sarsfield Barracks, having previously served with the 14th Infantry Battalion, and the 32nd Infantry Battalion. He is the author of *British Voices from the Irish War on Independence* and *Fighting for Dublin*. Corporal Sheehan has recently been awarded his PhD in History at Mary Immaculate College, University of Limerick.

Sergeant Michael Deegan currently serves as PDF cadre with the 31st Reserve Logistics Battalion in Sarsfield Barracks, having served with the 12th Battalion from 1985 to 2007. Sergeant Deegan has served overseas in Lebanon (twice), Yugoslavia, and Kosovo. He had recently been awarded a Masters in History at Mary Immaculate College, University of Limerick.

Private Denis Carroll currently serves with the 12th Battalion in Sarsfield Barracks, having joined the battalion in 1982. He previously served with the Naval Service from 1978 to 1982. Private Carroll was in fact born in married quarters in Sarsfield Barracks, when his father, Sergeant John Carroll, served there as a Medic with the No.1 Hospital Company.

Sergeant Stephen Kelly currently serves as PDF cadre with the 31st Reserve Military Police Company in Sarsfield Barracks. Sergeant Kelly has previously served with 2nd Field Artillery Regiment, the 29th Infantry Battalion, the 2nd Garrison Military Police Company, the 3rd Garrison Military Police Company, and the 1st Southern Brigade Military Police Company. He served two tours in the Lebanon. Sergeant Kelly established the Military Museum at Sarsfield Barrack, and is its curator.